To my five precious daughters:
Tracey, Launi, Fawn, Christy, and Gabrielle.

A special thanks to my editor, Lela Gilbert.

Most of all, thank you to Frank,
my Knight in Shining Armor.

**Other Books by
P.B. Wilson**

*Liberated Through Submission—
The Ultimate Paradox*

*Betrayal's Baby—
Turning the Bitter to Sweet*

KNIGHT in SHINING ARMOR

P. B. WILSON

HARVEST HOUSE PUBLISHERS
Eugene, Oregon 97402

KNIGHT IN SHINING ARMOR

Copyright © 1995 by P.B. Wilson
Published by Harvest House Publishers
Eugene, Oregon 97402

Library of Congress Cataloging-in-Publication Data

Wilson, P. B. (P. Bunny), 1950-
   Knight in shining armor / P.B. Wilson.
     p. cm.
   ISBN 1-56507-347-9
   1. Single women—Religious life. 2. Husbands—United States.
3. Marriage—Religious aspects—Christianity. I. Title.
BV4596.S5W55   1995
248.8' 432—dc20   95-11783
                                   CIP

Printed in the United States of America.

95   96   97   98   99   00   01 — 10 9 8 7 6 5 4 3 2 1

Contents

Acknowledgments

To my friends who have encouraged me and also given their valuable critiques. Thank you Christine, my sister Elenor, Marilyn, Sandi, Teresa, Lainie, Renee, Mattie, Mary, Virginia, Danette, Germaine, Carrie, Debra, Yvonne, Wendy, Katie, Sharon, Toni, Tina, Dina, Renee F., Melinda, and Tracy.

Knight Vision

Brimming with excitement, one of my single friends shared her vision with me. She is a woman I enjoy very much. She is committed to the Lord, faithful to her church, and has a servant's heart. Her news was exciting—God had revealed the man who would be her husband.

A week later another single friend recounted a similar experience. The Lord had also told her who her future husband would be. You can imagine my surprise when I discovered that both women were talking about the same man! Each one of them felt that God had shown them that their weddings would take place the same year with the same groom. As this book goes to press, neither woman has seen the vision come to pass.

Visions or Vain Imaginations?

That was not the first time I'd heard about a romantic "revelation" from God. My friend Priscilla's face glowed as she showed me a picture of the wedding gown she was making—along with the bridesmaids' dresses. She looked up and asked, "Would you be a bridesmaid in my wedding?"

"Sure," I responded. "When is the big day?"

She replied, "The first weekend in June."

I couldn't recall seeing Priscilla with a man at church during the past few months, so I inquired, "Who is the blessed gentleman? Do I know him?"

"No," she answered. "And he doesn't know about it yet, either."

Trying not to look confused, I said, "I don't understand. What do you mean he doesn't know about it yet?"

"The Lord showed me my wedding day, the man I'm going to marry, and then told me the date. I've rented the hall, hired a caterer and asked the women I want to be my brides-maids to participate. I know since God has revealed it to me,

He will reveal it to my future husband, too. I'm stepping out in faith because I know it will come to pass." Unfortunately for Priscilla, the only thing that came to pass was the wedding day. It came and went, but there was no wedding.

It is perfectly normal for a woman to dream of her "knight in shining armor." Even as little girls we rehearsed our weddings and visualized ourselves marching down the aisle, wearing a gown so beautiful that only the angels could have designed it.

But where is the fine line between dreams, fantasies, and godly visions? Are marriages made in heaven? Do we have a choice in who we select? Or has God already chosen our mate? Are we destined for one person only? As women, should we be passive or aggressive in securing the man of our dreams? As you read through this book, I hope you find the answers to these questions and more. For now, let's begin with the last question first.

The Manhunt

I am often asked by single women, "Should I become actively involved in looking for my husband or should I wait for him to find me?" Many who seek the answer to that question already know what the Bible says in Proverbs 18:22—

He who finds a wife finds what is good and receives favor from the LORD.

It's pretty clear that God has given to each male the challenge of seeking out his wife. In the Garden of Eden God said:

It is not good for the man to be alone. I will make a helper suitable for him (Genesis 2:18).

I believe that when God brought all the animals to Adam and he looked at them he was looking for a helper. But no suitable helper was found. While Adam slept, God fashioned the woman and brought her to him. Adam did his part by *looking* and God did His part by *bringing*.

The goal of this book is to allow God—not the world—to fashion you so the Lord can present you to your husband. Meanwhile, you can stop searching, stop visiting places where men hang out, stop waiting for supernatural revelations, and stop torturing yourself over when, where, and whether that special day will come. It will—in God's time and place—if you are properly prepared.

I recall when my day arrived. The telephone rang one morning and when I answered, a man named Frank asked to speak to my sister. They had gone out on a couple of dates. She wasn't in, so Frank and I carried on a light conversation. Out of the blue he asked, "So, how is your love life?"

I replied, "My love life is fantastic! I have someone who cares for me, is always there for me, and provides for me."

Frank said, "Well, I know a lot of people who live in Hollywood. Maybe I know him. What is his name?"

Without hesitation, I answered, "I don't know if you know Him or not. It's God."

Frank says that by the time he hung up the telephone he knew he was going to marry me. Only a few days before, his mother had been pressuring him to get married. Frank had told her, "Mom, I just can't find a woman who loves God." Fortunately, my sister was in love with another man, so a relationship between Frank and me didn't present a problem.

When Frank's call came, I wasn't looking for a husband; I was trusting in God as my Father. You can also be content, because God has a plan for your life, too.

The Desires of Our Hearts

Three observations led me to write this book. *First*, I've been astounded that so many sincere, Christian, single men throughout the country express a desire to marry but can't seem to find a suitable bride. *Second*, I've observed that a tremendous number of single women are at a loss knowing how to recognize a godly man. And *third,* through countless hours of counseling it has become evident that many couples are marrying for the wrong reasons. It is my hope to reach unmarried women *before* they say "I do"!

It may be helpful to have a friend work through this book with you. I've also provided some "Things to Think About and Do" at the end of each chapter to help you think through and evaluate the principles in that chapter.

Psalm 37:4 says, "Delight yourself in the LORD and he will give you the desires of your heart." If it is the desire of your heart to be married, God has a husband for you! Remember: *True desire is when we allow God to put His desires for us into our hearts.* So we must begin by developing our love relationship with the Lord.

Knight Blind

Since you are reading this book, I know there is a desire in your heart to be married. You may have joined the chorus of some other single women who complain, "There just aren't any good men around!" Well, be encouraged. You aren't going to be marrying *any good men*. You will be marrying *one good man*.

A single woman attending college in Washington, DC informed me that she'd heard a frightening statistic—supposedly there is only one man for every seven women. So she and a couple of her friends devised their own solution to the man shortage. They shared one man between three women! They all lived in the same apartment; they saw to his needs financially and he saw to their needs physically. Sounds like a perfect ungodly plan!

Don't be discouraged by worldly statistics. When God brings that one good man to you, you won't need to share him with anyone. In God's eyes, the equation changes every day. The options of who is available should not be based solely on what you see today. When people move, change jobs, lose a spouse, opportunities open up. On the face of this earth there is one man who will love you. God will present you to him at the right time. And until the right time arrives, there's plenty of work for you to be doing.

Under Construction

Have you ever taken a look through a peephole at a construction site? The old building has been demolished and a billboard illustrates how the new building will look. Meanwhile, there is a big hole in the ground where the new foundation is being laid. If you have the occasion to pass the site daily, you will notice that progress continues to take place even though you may not have a clue about what the construction crews are doing. Before long, the building will be ready for its intended purpose.

In order for this book to be effective, you need to take out your mental hammer, nails, and plywood. Build a wall around your life and hang out a sign that reads, "Under Construction for Six Months." Why six months? It takes about six months to get to know someone really well. And you'll want to spend that period of time with your True Husband:

> For your Maker is your husband—the LORD Almighty
> is his name—the Holy One of Israel is your Redeemer;
> he is called the God of all the earth (Isaiah 54:5).

Have you and the Lord been on your honeymoon? Have you spent as much time thinking about Him as you have thinking about "eligible" men? Do you remember meeting someone new and being consumed with thoughts and day-dreams about him? Well, if you have not enjoyed that kind of relationship with the Lord, it will be difficult for Him to do the construction work necessary to prepare you for your earthly husband.

The Lord wants to be our First Love. And that doesn't happen unless we have intimate fellowship with Him. He created us, loves us deeply, and desires us to know Him fully. He can't be our First Love if we focus all our emotional energy on another human. Once we are wholeheartedly committed to God, He is able to direct our steps, cover us with His peace, and give us the wisdom we need to make sound decisions. Then the Lord will expose the areas in our lives that need redesigning, rebuilding, or renovating.

Are you ready to start developing a close, intimate relationship with the Lord? Are you ready to let Him work with you in preparation for marriage?

If you are not seriously dating right now, I challenge you to wait until the full six months are over to begin. Even if you meet someone during the next six months who appears to be God's answer to your prayer, be careful. Satan will often send a counterfeit before the original arrives. Ask the gentleman to call you in six months because right now God has you under construction. If the gentleman is your man, he'll be there at the end of the wait. If you're currently thinking about getting married, please put a hold on your wedding date until you have finished the process in this book. Since you plan to be married for a lifetime, six months shouldn't seem like an unrealistic investment of your time.

By the way, don't assume that spending six months with God means spending every moment of every day in isolation! Look forward to enjoying the beauty of God's creation. You'll want to take trips to museums, zoos, national parks, and, perhaps, other countries. You'll discover new perspectives on life, new people, and new hobbies. The next six months promise to be among the best times of your life—you will be a new person by the end of this special time if you are committed to the process.

Before you begin, make your decision official. Please read the following commitment and then sign your name:

Lord, I want You to fashion me for my prospective husband. I commit the next six months of my life for Your construction. I will surrender any area which is not controlled by You so that my life will bring You glory.

_____ Date _____

If you don't feel you can sign this now, don't close the book! You'll have more time to think about it as you read further.

The Building

If you have ever stayed out of town overnight, you probably were careful about where your hotel was located. Were you concerned about the neighborhood? Was the appearance of the building important? Did you consider whether the hotel chain had a respectable reputation? I hope so.

When a man is trying to find a resting place, he will search for a building that appeals to him. Depending on the quality of the man, different kinds of building will catch his eye. Let's make sure the building you're erecting in your life will only attract a man of the highest caliber—someone who will respect and value who you are. That is why you are "under construction." You want your building to attract the appropriate type of person.

We all know women who seem to attract the wrong kind of men. They end a relationship with a man who is physically or verbally abusive. Then they go to a social gathering, and out of all the men in the room, they are drawn to someone who will abuse them again. Why do they constantly attract men who will reject them, who will insult them, or who are allergic to work and will not take the lead in making decisions? The reason may be that they have not learned to design, decorate, and dedicate their buildings to attract a godly man.

A Sure Foundation

Your building may be in pretty good shape with only a few cracks in need of repair. Or maybe you need to have a new foundation laid. No matter how wonderful your building looks, if the foundation is weak, life's storms will eventually cause the building to crumble. What is your foundation? What does your life rest upon?

Webster's Dictionary says a foundation is "a basis upon which something stands or is supported." What is holding you up? Have you knowingly, willingly, and sincerely asked Jesus Christ to come into your life?

In the book of Romans we find:

> If you confess with your mouth, "Jesus is Lord," and believe in your heart that God raised him from the dead, you will be saved (Romans 10:9).

If you believe the encyclopedia regarding the life of Jesus, it's history. If you believe that Jesus not only died but rose again for your sins, it's your salvation. It is only a prayer away. If you have not done so, ask Him to come into your life. When we believe Christ died for our sins and was resurrected to give us new life in Him, then He becomes the foundation of our lives.

> For no one can lay any foundation other than the one already laid, which is Jesus Christ (1 Corinthians 3:11).

> God's solid foundation stands firm, sealed with this inscription: "The Lord knows those who are his . . ." (2 Timothy 2:19).

Has the thought run through your mind, "What if I set aside six months to allow God to reconstruct me and I still don't meet my husband?" There's another necessary element to the construction of your character, and that is the growth of your personal faith.

Faith is being sure of what we hope for and certain of what we do not see (Hebrews 11:1).

We live by faith, not by sight (2 Corinthians 5:7).

Without faith it is impossible to please God (Hebrews 11:6).

Keep these Scriptures in your heart and meditate on them. Once you've laid a solid foundation, erected a sturdy building, and filled your rooms with understanding, knowledge, and wisdom, it will then be up to God to bring you to your husband.

Loving Jesus Daily

In my conversations with single women there is often frustration expressed over endless pressures which are faced on a daily basis. Once you get married, the pressures may differ, but they never leave. The solution for relief is the same for singles as it is for married people: rest on the firm foundation— the Lord.

A single woman who has learned this principle will carry it into her married life. When you add another person to your life, pressures increase. Some of you may be thinking, "I'll gladly take on the pressures of married life; just give me some *new* pressures!" Don't worry—you'll have your chance!

I married my Knight in Shining Armor in 1973. Since that time, we've had our share of challenges. But, because we apply God's Word to our marriage, we are experiencing the joy of being "one flesh" in all aspects of our lives. Nevertheless— although I love Frank with a passion—the first thing I think about upon awakening in the morning is Jesus. The last thing I think about before I go to sleep is Jesus. And throughout the day my thoughts drift to the Lord and His Word.

When I do think about Frank, I smile and tell God how grateful I am that He brought him into my life, but then my thoughts once again go to the Lord. When I was single, the process was the same: I was consumed by thoughts of my Divine Father who watched over me.

What do you think about all day? Start in the morning and pay close attention as your day unfolds. Most women agree that during the day their thoughts drift toward career, money, family, friends, and, of course, toward themselves. How we view ourselves and our God in light of those issues determines the strength of our foundation.

Let's look at three areas that call for a very strong foundation: money, relationships, and trust.

A Provider You Can Count On

A single parent said to me, "My children think money grows on trees. I am so stressed just trying to make ends meet and having to explain why they can't have designer jeans like the other children. I'm tired of carrying this load."

Money is a vital issue in life, whether we're single or married. But the best time to stretch your money muscles is when you're single. Finances are one of the primary reasons for divorce, so getting priorities established now will help you select a mate with compatible values. Have you ever thought about how wonderful it would be to have a husband who is your provider? Someone who will help carry the load, or at least relieve it a little? Maybe you should think twice.

When I married Frank, he was a successful record producer earning a six-figure income. A year after our marriage, we recommitted our lives to Christ. Two years later, Frank's recording contract expired and needed to be renewed. He refused to do so because he didn't want to be locked into a deal that would limit his ability to pursue God's will for his life. Since he wasn't sure what God wanted Him to do, he walked away from the music industry for over a year while waiting to hear from the Lord. During that time, our income virtually came to a halt. This didn't happen because Frank was slothful or uncaring. He was waiting on God.

If I'd gone into the marriage believing that Frank was my provider, I probably would not have been able to endure the crisis. But it became one of the highlights of our marriage. We had weekly Bible studies with our friends, we spent quality time together, and we rested in the Lord.

Financial fortunes often change—sometimes dramatically. Loss of revenue can happen to anyone.

A news reporter showed a video of a handsome young man who had been married just a week. He was well-educated with a good paying job. As the video of the wedding continued, the newscaster described a tragic turn of events. The groom had been in a hit-and-run accident and would be permanently paralyzed from the neck down. His bride would now be providing for herself *and* her invalid husband for the rest of her life.

One of the greatest lessons you can learn *before* you get married is that your future husband will never be your provider. God can use him as a *provision*, but the Lord alone is our *Provider*. God can also use you as a provider. Sometimes more money may flow through you than through your spouse. In any case, we should never lose sight of where our resources really come from. As you learn to entrust your single life to God as your Provider, that confidence in Him will carry on into marriage.

God's Economy Sheet

Some of you may be thinking, "Well, if God is my Provider, where is the money?"

Money comes in different forms: income, gifts-in-kind, and savings. God has his own ledger sheet. I call it "God's Economy." Take out a piece of paper so I can help you understand how wealthy you are. Draw three columns.

At the top of one, put *Income.*

On the second, write *Gifts-in-Kind.*

On the third, write *Savings.*

Under the income heading, write your monthly earnings minus taxes, minus your 10 percent tithe. (You do pay tithes, don't you? If not, it will directly affect the other two columns.)

In the second column, entitled *Gifts-in-Kind,* write down goods or services that God gave you through other people. Include the approximate dollar amount. For example, you moved into a new apartment and the manager waived your security deposit of $200. Or, your hairdresser may have told you she wanted to style your hair for free instead of charging you $40. Someone may have blessed you with a new $60 jacket for one of your teenagers. If your mind is blank, be observant over the next month and write down each gift when it arrives.

When you come to the third column, *Savings,* you might think, "This certainly doesn't apply to me!" Yes, it does. What has God saved you from? Suppose you or your child were stricken with a catastrophic illness. What would the hospital bill have been? What would it cost to replace your car if it was stolen? How much would it cost to replace your valuables if your home was burglarized? Most of all, what if you were disabled and could not earn the money listed in the first column?

By now you're getting the picture! Money is not only what we earn, it is also what is given and what is not taken away. When I prepared my list, I discovered I was a very rich woman. If you are stressed over money, there is a good chance you have not checked God's Economy Sheet.

First Things First

Earlier I mentioned that if you are not paying a ten percent tithe on the money you earn, it could affect your *Gifts-in-Kind* and *Savings.* These two areas are extra blessings from God, and He is not likely to abundantly bless a robber. Are you a robber? Let's look at Malachi 3:8-9:

> Will a man rob God? Yet you rob me. But you ask, "How do we rob you?" In tithes and offerings. You are under a curse . . . because you are robbing me.

I think it's pretty safe to say that God does not need our money. One of the purposes of tithing is to keep our financial focus clear. When we give ten percent of our income to the church, it is our way of saying, "God, your gift of health and strength enabled me to earn this money, and I thank You. I give to you ten percent in recognition of the 100 percent you gave me."

God's reply is:

> "Test me in this," says the LORD Almighty, "and see if I will not throw open the floodgates of heaven and pour out so much blessing that you will not have room enough for it" (Malachi 3:10).

In laying a solid foundation for your future, it is important that you put to rest the issue of money. God is our Provider. Your Knight in Shining Armor should not be chosen solely for the amount of money he makes. In fact, if you don't feel like the richest woman on earth there is more work to do on your foundation. You may also need to make some adjustments on how you spend the money God gives you.

Many of our spending woes come because we've demonstrated a lack of good judgment, perhaps by overextending ourselves with credit. My pastor says, "If your out-go exceeds your income then your upkeep will be your downfall!" The time to fix your money situation is during your single life. Good biblical money principles will follow you into your marriage, and your husband will appreciate it more than you know.

If you need help to set up or work on a budget, I recommend *The Money Book* by Mahlon Hetrick (Barbour and Co.).

Building Healthy Relationships

Moving on from monitoring our thoughts concerning money, our next assignment is to reflect on our relationships with friends and family. I loved the Lord for ten years before He challenged me concerning the bitterness in my heart toward a particular family member. With the Lord's help, I was able to get free of the bondages of bitterness and it stimulated me to write a book entitled *Betrayal's Baby*. Many of our betrayals take place in our families.

Recently a woman told me, "One of my sisters shared her heart one day. She said there was a spirit of unforgiveness in our family among the women. I am close to 50 years old and had never realized that fact. Now I know why it is so hard for me to forgive."

Stand back and consider your thoughts as they pass through your mind. Are they pleasant? Or do they cause you anguish? If they are pleasant, keep them. If they are despairing, purpose in your heart to change them. If you haven't learned to enjoy peaceful and loving relationships with the family you already have, how can you expect to get along with a husband and his family? You can be sure that your Knight and your future in-laws will be just as imperfect as your own next of kin. Be faithful in forgiving and loving the people God has placed in your life.

The same is true of friends. Have you ever had a close friend or roommate who hurt you in some way? Did you put up a wall of defense? Did you develop a spirit of distrust toward people? That kind of hostile response will flow into your marriage. We need to make sure our foundation is based on trust. However, our trust is not supposed to be placed in men and women, but in God as He directs our lives. The moment we put our trust in a human being the Bible says we are cursed:

> Cursed is the one who trusts in man, who depends on
> flesh for his strength and whose heart turns away from
> the LORD. He will be like a bush in the wastelands. . . .
> He will dwell in the parched places of the desert . . .
> (Jeremiah 17:5,6).

I have been hurt by friends, too—but only because my trust was in them instead of in God. I brought the pain upon myself. When I realized I had violated God's law, I repented before the Father and began loving again. For God's Word says

> But blessed is the man who trusts in the LORD, whose
> confidence is in him. He will be like a tree planted by
> the water . . . (Jeremiah 17:7,8).

A Matter of Trust

The matter of trust includes the man you will eventually call your husband. Although you will need to be able to trust him as far as human honesty and integrity are concerned, he can't be given a position in your life that will diminish your absolute trust and confidence in God. Many women wrap themselves around the man they love and re-create themselves to fit his preferences. They begin to eat what he eats, like what he likes, and think what he thinks. Although it's normal to adapt to a boyfriend or husband, avoid a man who thinks the construction work is his job.

A woman can't afford to trust him, instead of God, to mold her personality or to remake her into his image.

If you invest six months in knowing God more intimately, you will come to know yourself more clearly, too. The self-respect you gain by recognizing yourself as God's beloved will help keep you from making unwise compromises about who you are when your "knight" appears. This is why it's important to let your Maker do six months of construction work *before* you begin to date someone new.

Trust the Lord to do what is right in your life. Don't consecrate the next six months to the Lord solely because you desire a husband. Do it because you know it's right to develop a deep and abiding relationship with the Lord. We've all heard Christians say, "God has never failed me yet!" He won't fail you, either. Let Him teach you to trust Him with every aspect of your life.

God gives His best to those
Who leave the choice to Him.

_____ *Things to Think About and Do* _____

1) Make sure you're resting on a solid foundation. Have you accepted Jesus into your life?

2) Start a personal six-month journal. Record your observations and new discoveries about yourself and others often.

3) Monitor and summarize in your journal your daily thoughts concerning family, friends, and finances. Begin to memorize Scriptures that will counteract any negative thinking. One wise woman carried verses on 3 x 5 cards and called them "counter cards." She used them to counteract negative thoughts.

4) Place an asterisk beside every thought listed above in which you see improvement on a daily basis.

Good Knight

Sheila is beautiful, successful, and sincere. She has suffered two failed marriages and is now involved in another dead-end relationship. She is well-aware that she has a pattern of attracting the wrong kind of men, but doesn't know how to break the cycle. When she talked to me, she was open and willing to do whatever was suggested. I asked her about a particular gentleman who is part of our inner circle of friends. Like Sheila, he possesses wonderful attributes and is a good-looking man. They have been close friends for years.

"Sheila," I questioned, "have you ever considered dating Don?"

She chuckled and said, "Never! He's not my type."

I asked Sheila to make a list of everything she wanted in a husband. Then I encouraged her to place Don's name at the top of the page and check off every criteria he met. What do you think happened? He earned a 95 out of 100 score!

Do you remember when the men walked with Jesus after He had risen from the dead? They didn't even recognize Him and they were face to face, holding a conversation. It was as if a veil was hiding his identity. Is your future husband veiled by your unrealistic expectations? While you have frantically been looking around for an available gentleman, is it possible that you already know your Knight in Shining Armor? Let's find out.

What is your type? Tall or short, heavy or thin, intense or playful? Have you ever seen a small group of men gathered together and decided, before one of them even approached you, which one you would be interested in? In the same situation, many of us would have overlooked Jesus:

> He had no beauty or majesty to attract us to him,
> nothing in his appearance that we should desire him
> (Isaiah 53:2).

According to this Scripture, Jesus was an ordinary-looking man. We might not have noticed him in a crowd. Yet what man could have loved us more? God could have given Jesus any kind of appearance He chose, but He did not make him dramatically attractive. It's clear that outward beauty was not God's main focus:

> The LORD does not look at the things man looks at.
> Man looks at the outward appearance, but the LORD
> looks at the heart (1 Samuel 16:7).

I can hear your thoughts: "Oh great. She's trying to tell me that my future husband is going to be unattractive!" No, he may be the most physically handsome man in the world. I'm sure there are some women reading this book who have dated a few movie-star types. But if a man's heart is not right, he becomes an ugly person all too quickly. As the film character Forrest Gump paraphrased, "Pretty is as pretty does."

Finding the Right Kind of Man

To discount a man because of his outer appearance may cost you your second greatest blessing (the first is Jesus). When I met Frank, I was drawn more to his character than his appearance. He was not my usual type. However, after 21 years there is no man in the universe more handsome to me than my husband. Love reshapes our vision.

How do we develop our taste for a certain type of man? When did we decide a man had to have a certain kind of look and personality for us to be interested? In his book, *The Three Battlegrounds*, Francis Frangipane says:

> The soul is the combination of "mind, will and emotions." . . . Generally speaking, the essence of who we are is made of events and how we responded to those events. Who we are today is the sum of what we have encountered in life and our subsequent reactions. Abuses and afflictions hammer us one way, encouragement and praise inflate us another. Our reaction to each event, whether positive or negative, is poured into the creative marrow of our individuality, where it is blended into the nature of our character. With a few exceptions, those events which we remember the most have shaped us the most. Although the events of our lives are irreversible, our *reactions* to those events can still be changed. And as our reactions change, we change (Advancing Church Publications, 1989).

And, I might add, as we change, so our choice in who we will spend the rest of our life changes also. Let's study your type. List below everything you want in a husband.

1)

2)

3)

4)

5)

6)

7)

8)

9)

10)

Now go back over that list. Next to everything you can do without write "WDW" (willing to do without). That will leave you with the essentials. However, there are a couple of points that *must* be on the list. First and foremost, is he a man that doesn't want to break God's heart? Notice I didn't say, "A man that goes to church, studies, and knows the Scriptures." That's important, of course. However, many of the couples we counsel who are seriously considering divorce attend church faithfully and can quote Scripture. True spirituality requires more than that. When you find a man who is saddened when he disappoints God, you have found a gem. If he doesn't want to hurt God, he won't intentionally hurt you, because that would hurt God.

Besides being unwilling to hurt God, he must be a man with a vision. What does he believe God has called him to do with his life?

> Where there is no vision, the people perish (Proverbs 29:18 KJV).

That Scripture certainly includes marriages. It is of the utmost importance to know a man's vision. If he feels God has called him to live in the mountains to work with indigenous people and you're afraid of heights, he is probably not destined to be your husband.

We can change the "type" of man we are attracted to. Take the time to really consider the qualities you are looking for in a mate. I suspect that, whatever your list is today, when you finish this book, you'll discover that some of the essentials have changed.

I often ask single women to tell me about their dating experiences. Although dating can be enjoyable, I've heard many horror stories about past relationships. However, as terrible as those situations may have been, it's even more frightening to women when I suggest that they consider changing the type of man they want. The very thought places them in unfamiliar territory. How can a woman change such an integral part of herself? How can you become the right woman for the man of God's choosing? If you aren't changed on the inside, you may not be able to recognize your Knight in Shining Armor—even when he is looking directly into your eyes.

What We Can Learn from Esther

The story of Esther gives everyone hope—particularly the single woman. If you have never taken the time to read and enjoy this Bible book of only ten chapters, please indulge yourself. We can learn a lot from Esther. Esther probably never imagined herself as the wife of the king. And even if she had, the chances were slim she would ever become a queen, considering her background and circumstances. And yet, with the right kind of help, the impossible happened.

The story begins with King Xerxes (Ahasuerus), who ruled over 127 provinces from Ethiopia to India. His palace was in Susa. One day the king decided to throw a party for the nobility of each province. The party lasted six months! When it was over, he held another week-long party in the palace garden for everyone great and small (probably as a reward for six months of service to hundreds of people!).

On the last day of that second party, the drunken king asked the seven eunuchs who served him to bring Vashti, the queen, to the garden to show off her beauty.

Vashti was having a party in her own palace at the time, and when the eunuchs expressed the king's wishes, the queen refused to cooperate. She turned Xerxes down. (In those days, his request was humiliating and disrespectful to her.) Returning to the king, the eunuchs reported Vashti's answer. Xerxes became outraged. He counseled with the wise men in his court and they suggested that he send the queen away and never see her again. In his drunken state he accepted their suggestion.

However, the story goes on to tell us that when he was no longer mad, he began to miss his beautiful queen. Seeing his dilemma, the wise men suggested that he select another queen from among the many beautiful virgins in his 127 provinces. The virgins would be brought to Susa, to the palace, to be prepared by the king's chief eunuch of women, Hegai. (A eunuch was a man who had been castrated so he would be chaste among the king's women.) The preparation process took one year. (Count your blessings—you're only setting aside six months!)

A proclamation went forth across the kingdom. Among the hundreds of women who arrived was Esther. She was being raised by her cousin Mordecai because both of her parents were deceased. When Hegai saw Esther, we read that he liked what he saw. Whatever she did or said, Hegai saw that she had the potential to become the queen.

Based on the number of virgins there must have been, I think it's safe to assume that Hegai was not the only eunuch working with the women, but he was in charge. How do you think he got that position? Obviously he had done a great job in preparing other women for the king. He was the best. And in Esther, Hegai saw something he was sure would please the king. He assigned Esther seven of the best maids to train her, and he housed her in the choicest room.

The selection of Esther is fascinating because, in many ways, she was least likely to become queen. It seems more reasonable that Hegai would select one of the virgins who had come from a noble family. Surely he could have found someone who had already graduated from the local John Robert Powers Modeling School and was accustomed to high society living. He would have saved himself months of preparation work. I believe that Esther not only had the appearance that Hegai knew would please the king, but she also possessed a teachable spirit. Hegai may have figured that if Esther was chosen, she would take him into her palace to serve her for the rest of her life. There was a lot riding on Hegai's choice, and in choosing Esther, he had his work cut out for him.

In order for Esther to become queen she had to overcome three enormous obstacles:

1) her past

2) her present

3) her future

Coming to Terms with the Past

Let's imagine the scene as hundreds of virgins poured in from the king's 127 provinces. In those days, Middle Eastern people didn't travel without their families. It must have been a sight to see the caravans arriving. The rich would have owned the finest camels, draped in tapestries and gold. There would also have been middle-class, poor, and slave virgins. The only requirements to qualify as a contender for queen were beauty and virginity. But no matter what the virgin's status, most of them would have arrived with their parents. Can't you see the fathers with their chests stuck out proudly, and the mothers crying over the thought of saying goodbye to their beautiful daughters?

Now Esther's parents were deceased and she was being raised by her cousin, Mordecai. How do you think Esther felt at the sight of those other virgins? She was probably overwhelmed with jealousy and envy. Why had life treated her so harshly? She could have tortured herself with questions that could never be answered. Yet we know Esther was not angry and bitter.

How do we know about Esther's attitude? The Bible says that she won Hegai's favor. You've probably known people who are depressed about their lives. An ominous cloud hangs over them and manifests itself in an unattractive attitude. And yet Esther had pleased Hegai. She had apparently come to grips with her past and her personality reflected it.

. . .

What about your past? Are you angry, bitter, unforgiving, or resentful? Do you wonder over and over again why life seems to have treated you so unfairly? Unless you have given the pain and loss to God, and have accepted it as part of God's plan for your life, you will bring a victim's attitude into your future marriage.

Living in the Present

In addition to her tragic past, there is another reason Esther would have been the least likely to become queen. Consider where she lived. Hundreds of the empire's beautiful virgins traveled to Susa from as far away as Ethiopia and India. But Esther could walk from her home to the house where the beautiful women would be prepared!

Esther lived with her cousin in Susa where he held the lowly position of doorkeeper at the palace gate. And that was probably a distinct disadvantage to Esther. It's reasonable to assume that she would have to unlearn everything she had been taught regarding deference to royalty. In preparing to become queen, she would have to stop looking down when nobility walked by; she would instead learn to raise her eyes to look directly at the nobles as equals. She would have to learn to turn with her head held high and float to the door with the greatest of ease. Let's not forget that, if she failed to act with the proper deference, the consequences could be severe. Imagine how *hard* it would be to break a habit that, if violated, may have carried specific disgraceful punishments. Fortunately, Esther learned.

I can hear Hegai the eunuch, raising his voice as Esther continued to make the same mistakes over and over again—

actions that had become second nature to her. She must have cried many tears in her pillow. Knowing how vindicative jealous women can be, imagine what it was like when she was in the company of the other virgins. Those of blue-blood families probably fumed at Hegai's decision to prepare the ward of a lowly doorkeeper to become queen. Their comments must have been quite cutting. Meanwhile, the slave girls probably never failed to remind Esther of her lowly position in life. Interestingly enough, Scripture says that Esther was so beautiful she eventually won the favor of all the other virgins. She must have been an amazing woman.

• • •

What is your present situation? How many of life's experiences have caused you to stare at the floor in shame—to back out of a room in disgrace? What type of men have you attracted into your life over the years? Esther gives hope that, no matter what your present and past situations have been, you can overcome and change the direction of your life.

Fears About the Future

Like the rest of us, Esther didn't know what her future held. Out of the hundreds of virgins who had come to the palace, the king would select only one. Could she dare to believe she would actually become queen? Wouldn't the king recognize her as the ward of one of the doorkeepers? What if she forgot to hold her head up and look into his eyes? These questions, and many others, would have challenged Esther's confidence. She had to believe in herself despite her past and present situation. And no one could help her with her thoughts about the future. It was a battle she fought alone. We know she won because the king chose her to be his queen.

In chapter 1, we talked about the importance of our thought life. You, like Esther, have the ability to control your thoughts and believe that, in your future, God's plans for you will be fulfilled.

Pleasing the King

I tried to picture what it was like the day Esther was summoned to meet the king. She submitted herself completely to Hegai's instructions. Can you envision her being led to the king's chambers, beautifully attired from head to foot and surrounded by his guard? Her heart must have been pounding in her chest. I can imagine the king sitting on his throne with his chin in his hand thinking, "Another night, another woman. I hope she doesn't talk me to death like the one last night. Or try to give me all the reasons why she should be my queen."

When the doors swung open and Esther stood as an angel before him, I see him sitting straight in his chair and thinking to himself, "Vashti?" Of course it couldn't be her. But the way in which she carried herself no doubt reminded him of the queen he had deeply loved.

> The king loved Esther above all the women, and she obtained grace and favour in his sight more than all the virgins; so that he set the royal crown upon her head, and made her queen instead of Vashti (Esther 2:17 KJV).

Fairy tales may not always come true, but God's plan surely will.

Overcoming the Odds

Perhaps you're wondering what the story of Esther has to do with you and your search for your Knight. In actual fact, you and I and every other believer in God have a lot in common with Esther. There are three similarities that stand out:

1. *Esther was lowly born.* She had to overcome the habits of a lifetime—attitudes and training—to move with ease among royalty.

> But thanks be to God, that though you used to be slaves to sin, you wholeheartedly obeyed the form of teaching to which you were entrusted. You have been set free from sin and have become slaves to righteousness (Romans 6:17,18).

2. *Esther had to meet two qualifications.* She had to be beautiful and she had to be a virgin. In a similar sense, there are also only two qualifications for us to become adopted into God's royal family:

> If you confess with your mouth, "Jesus is Lord," and believe in your heart that God raised him from the dead, you will be saved (Romans 10:9).

3. *Esther had a wonderful instructor.* Hegai was her patient, dedicated teacher. Who do you have to fashion you for your Knight?

> But the Counselor, the Holy Spirit, whom the Father will send in my name, will teach you all things and remind you of everything I have said to you (John 14:26).

Just as Hegai knew how to please the king, the Holy Spirit knows exactly what it takes to please the Lord. He is more than willing to teach you what to do. He will be God's instrument in fashioning you into the woman God wants you to be, and to prepare you to be a godly and loving wife. Remember, you will need to submit to Him as Esther did to Hegai. There is no way this will happen without spending quality time developing a close relationship with the Father, Son, and Holy Spirit. When that happens, God will be able to direct your steps. He will make the changes in you that will allow you to be attracted to the kind of man He has in mind for you.

The Importance of Preparation

I personally know the value of being fashioned *before* marriage and not after. In my case, I wasn't aware of a book I could read that would carry me through vital steps of preparation. And so I carried my own personal form of bondage into my marriage. You might be thinking, "But everything turned out all right for you."

You're right, but only at a tremendous price paid by myself, my husband, and our children. If I had known I could be free of my painful experiences *before* marriage, I would have done everything in my power to overcome the past. Fortunately, "All things God works together for the good of those who love him, who have been called according to his purpose" (Romans 8:28). God has chosen to use my difficult experiences to help others. And I am grateful that Frank was strong enough to endure the constant assaults launched from my crippled character. It took approximately ten years for me to break through to the other side. And that's a long time— longer than the six months I hope you're willing to invest.

Erasing Past Criticism

In the beginning, much of my behavior seemed shrouded in mystery. I remember going to pieces each time Frank expressed the tiniest criticism. I can hear myself shouting, "You never say anything good about me. All you notice is what I do wrong!" Frank knew this was not true. For years he was puzzled at my outbursts until he put two and two together, and began to understand me.

I grew up in an environment where it seemed that my mother thought that the way to improve me was to point out all my faults. I was not yelling at Frank when he criticized me, I was yelling at my mother who was not present. I was a slave to my past, and I didn't know it. Listen to God's Word:

> Do not judge, or you too will be judged. For in the same way you judge others, you will be judged (Matthew 7:1,2).

When I sat in judgment of my mother for being too critical, I didn't realize that the same characteristic was attaching itself to me. I was in desperate need of approval, yet was unable to give it to my husband or children. I could only see what was happening to me; I was blind to how I was affecting others. The Holy Spirit had to teach me how to break the vicious cycle of my past through forgiveness, reconciliation, and unconditional love. It wasn't easy. Sometimes I felt as if life itself was being sucked away from me. Nevertheless, I obeyed the Holy Spirit's leading, broke the curse, and now I am free to love my husband, children, and friends.

Moving Beyond the Past

But that wasn't my only problem. When I was growing up, I was told that sex was a marital duty. There was no way for me to know the tremendous impact that lie would have on my life. Who wants to perform a duty?

I also had an explosive temper. One day, in exasperation, I hit Frank in the chest as hard as I could. I thank God I married a man who had been taught never to hit a woman. I was raging, and Frank was usually the person who received the full brunt of my sin. I continuously blamed him for my condition. Somehow he just seemed to "bring the devil out in me." I didn't realize the value of the friend I had.

My mother was also a compulsive cleaner. While growing up, our house was immaculate. House-cleaning for her meant pulling out the stove and wiping behind it. She changed our clothes three times a day and the washer and dryer were always going. I don't fault her for this; I am grateful for her diligence. I did notice, however, that she was too tired to give her attention to my father. That caused a series of problems.

Since I wasn't as compulsive as my mother, once again I sat in judgment and reaped the results. Although I did not clean to the same extent, the spirit of busyness had attached itself to me. For years, whenever Frank drove in the driveway or walked into a room, I would jump up and begin to do something. I didn't want him to see me not busy. About ten years into our marriage, Frank found me sitting on the sofa watching TV. I quickly said, "I just sat down two minutes ago."

He turned to me and asked, "Why did you say that?"

Taken aback, I answered, "Well, I didn't want you to think I was just sitting around all day."

"Bunny," he replied, "you work hard. You deserve to rest whenever you feel like it."

From that day forward, I stopped jumping up when Frank came home. It took great effort, but I finally worked through it.

Some of these examples may seem petty to you, but they completely controlled my life and actions. They took a terrible toll on my marriage, and if Frank wasn't the patient and forgiving man he is, I'm not sure our marriage would have survived. I hope you will allow God to make these kinds of changes in your life before your Knight appears. I pray that you'll realize, as you continue to read, that God may have an earthly "king" in mind for you, but unless you allow Him to prepare you to be the right kind of "queen," you'll miss out on a glorious future.

Now It's Your Turn!

Just as Esther gave her undivided attention to Hegai so that she could be prepared to become royalty, you also have the opportunity, under the instruction of the Holy Spirit, to be fashioned for your husband. And, like Esther's, your training process won't be easy.

If you have been verbally or physically abused, people may not be able to see it with the human eye. But there is a good chance your self-image is looking down at the floor. I can hear the Holy Spirit saying, "Lift your eyes up. You are royalty. You are a joint heir to the throne of Christ" (see 1 Peter 3:7). Don't you know that there is never a time God is not thinking about you? His thoughts of you outnumber the grains of sand (Psalms 139:17,18).

The Holy Spirit is going to say it over and over again until you change your habits. It will take everything within you to break the bondage placed on you by the world, the flesh, and the devil.

You may have determined to never marry or remarry because of painful past experiences. And yet the Holy Spirit knows your hidden desire. He will challenge you, "Don't you want someone to love you as Christ loved the church?" (see Ephesians 5:25). "There is a good man for you but I need to fix your eyes so you will recognize him. Take your guard down and allow yourself to become vulnerable. I will lead you." You will learn more about the Holy Spirit in Chapter 5.

Shameful experiences in your past may cause your spirit to back out of rooms hoping no one will see you—experiences such as abortion, rape, incest, or homosexuality. Your best friend and teacher, the Holy Spirit, would probably say, "When you confess and repent of anything you've done wrong, your heavenly Father throws your sins into a sea of forgetfulness. If He can forgive you, why can't you forgive yourself? Your heavenly Father is a God of second (and more) chances. You are no longer a slave to your sins or your past. But the bondage can only be broken if you believe it."

A divorced friend once told me, "I don't believe I should expect the best in a husband because of the mistakes I have made in life. In the church where I was raised people just didn't get divorces. I was the first in my family."

I imagined the Lord nodding and then responding, "I know all about that. They are right in saying that I hate divorce. But they are wrong to say that divorce cannot be forgiven. Don't you remember the woman caught in adultery? The love and forgiveness I poured upon her not only released her from shame, but convicted everyone who accused her. Who are you going to believe? Your friends and relatives or your Father in heaven?"

Mirror, Mirror on the Wall

Esther was prepared externally as well as internally for her encounter with her future husband. She went through a beautification process that made her look like a queen. During your six months of preparation, you'll want to focus your attention on your outward appearance, too.

It is sometimes natural for us to use magazine covers as guidelines for beauty, but this is a mistake. Everything, everyone God made is uniquely beautiful. When you look in the mirror, what do you see? Are you beautiful? If your answer is "No!" or "A little . . ." we have a lot of work to do! When God made you, He said "It is good." Your first step toward true beauty is to agree with God. Your second step is to make the most of the gifts he has given you.

A clean body is a must, followed by teeth that are regularly cleaned. Oh, I know you hate the dentist, but it's necessary for you to have healthy gums and a beautiful smile.

Esther was given special baths that relaxed her and left her fragrant and soft-skinned (Esther 2:12). Do you have a bathtub? Why not put it to use over the next six months. Bubble baths and oil baths don't cost a lot of money, but they will calm you, pamper you, and make you feel like a queen.

As you start from the top of your body and move down, you'll also want to consider:

- your hair (cleanness, style, color, and health)
- your makeup (remember the goal is to enhance, not to cover up)

- your weight (you can accomplish a lot in six months)
- your clothes (even your underwear)
- your shoes (polished and repaired)

While you are focused on your external appearance, don't forget to keep your budget in mind. In reality, little changes can make a big difference. For example, you may not be able to afford a new wardrobe, but accessories like scarves, earrings, pins, and necklaces can add attractive touches to the things you already own.

Modesty is a must when it comes to dressing for your Knight. Christian women have to be careful of clothing that is too tight, too short, too low in the front, or too skimpy in the back. As the old saying goes, "If it's not for sale, take the sign down!"

Each day the Holy Spirit will commend you on your progress and expose areas in which you need to grow. He may also reveal to you the existence of some specific wounds that will require further attention (we'll talk more about that in the next chapter). If you allow the Holy Spirit to become as real to you as Hegai the eunuch was to Esther, he will prepare you for your ultimate meeting with your Knight in Shining Armor.

_____ *Things to Think About and Do* _____

1) Ask the Holy Spirit to reveal the three greatest areas in your life that need to be healed, for example, overcoming bitterness, fear, doubt, jealousy, anger, etc. List them below:

a)

b)

c)

2) If you do not own a concordance, please borrow or purchase one from your Christian bookstore.

A concordance allows you to select a word—such as anger, fear, doubt—and helps you locate every Scripture listed in the Bible that includes that word. Once you've obtained a concordance, write down every Scripture that relates to the three areas of difficulty in your life.

3) Memorize those Scriptures. Meditate on particular passages that stand out to you and allow the Holy Spirit to shine His light in the dark areas of your life.

4) Make a list of some financially feasible ways you can make yourself more attractive for your Knight.

———————————————————————

3

Knight Time

Most unmarried women look forward to the day they will be able to spend endless hours of quality time with their Knight in Shining Armor. They look forward to companionship, shared experiences, and intimate conversations. In their dreams, all those empty days of loneliness are gone forever. And yet, the loneliest women I have ever met are married!

You see, when you're single, you expect to be lonely. But when you're married to the man of your dreams and your communication has failed—along with your sex life—that's even greater loneliness. Loneliness is when you can't talk to him; when he won't talk to you; when it seems as if you're beginning to share nothing in common but the kids, the house, and the car. How many married couples do you know who are like two ships passing in the night?

Before I wrote this book, I went to a Christian bookstore to check out the available material written for singles. I was astonished to see so little in print. When I inquired as to the reason for the shortage, I was informed that most singles are unhappy with their status and are not interested in becoming a "better single." Essentially, unmarried men and women are in a holding pattern, waiting for their long-awaited wedlock to take flight.

The fact is, in order to be happily married, you must become happily single. You have to become "Me" before you can successfully become "We." Furthermore, no matter who we marry, Jesus must continue to be the lover of our soul. If we are looking to another human to meet needs that only God can fulfill, we will be utterly disappointed. God will give us the desire of our hearts, but we are first required to delight ourselves in Him.

Specific Healing

In chapter 1 you started to keep a journal, monitor your thoughts, and memorize Scriptures that would demolish any negative thinking. In chapter 2, the truth of God's redeeming power was shared through the story of Esther. No matter what unpleasantness your past or present situation may involve, God can change it as you yield to the leadership of the Holy Spirit.

But while you're dealing with the past and the present, you may discover that there are certain areas of your life that require specific healing. If so, this should happen before your wedding day. Let's look at another woman in the Bible who overcame obstacles that were trying to destroy her. If you are willing to follow in her footsteps, you too can be set free of wounds that may be subtly draining your life away.

Most people have heard the story of the woman who had an issue of blood (hemorrhaging) for twelve years (see Mark 5:25-34). Leviticus 15:19-25 describes the Jewish custom of dealing with a woman who had an issue of blood. During those days, when a woman had her monthly cycle, she was treated much like a leper. She was required to go to a camp outside the city for seven days, go through a cleansing process, and then return home. If anyone sat or lay down in a place where she had been, or if any person touched her, he or she also became defiled and had to go through a cleansing process. Occasionally a woman would continue to bleed beyond the days of her normal menstrual cycle. Here's what the Scripture tells us about that:

> When a woman has a discharge of blood for many days at a time other than her monthly period or has a discharge that continues beyond her period, she will be unclean as long as she has the discharge, just as in the days of her period (Leviticus 15:25).

Now, before we continue, I would like you to take out your Bible and read Mark 5:25-34. Once you've read the story for yourself, please allow me to share what I've discovered in it.

I believe the Scriptures tell us a great deal about this nameless woman. It seems she was a woman, not a teenager. Apparently she was wealthy. How do I know this? She had been seeing physicians for twelve years, and she was just running out of money. When was the last time you went to see a doctor? I don't have to tell you that it's an expensive investment to keep seeking medical help for twelve long years. We usually go to doctors until we are convinced they are not providing a cure. And despite this woman's efforts, and her physicians', she was not getting any better.

The Scriptures also suggest that she very much wanted to return to whatever she'd been forced to leave behind when she started to bleed. As we read in Leviticus, she would have grown accustomed to going outside the city during her monthly cycle. However, once she began to bleed constantly, her whole world changed. At some point, she left the city expecting to be back in a week. She wasn't allowed to return for more than a decade. What did this woman leave behind?

- *She left her family.* During this historical period, single people did not live alone. Even widows were taken into someone's home. I think it's safe to assume she had family. Did she have a mother she could no longer hug and kiss? Or a father she was unable to meet at the city gate when he returned home from a business trip? What about holding her nieces and nephews? If she was married, she may have had children of her own.

- *She left her friends.* Did they come to visit? How long do you think they continued to do so? Even if she had one loyal friend, can you see how difficult it would have been for her to listen to this woman's troubles year after year? Can you imagine how hard it would have been to support her in her quest for healing?

- *She left her husband or boyfriend.* Was she married, or did she have her eye on a particular gentleman in the city? Either way, her dreams were tragically disrupted. Did she have to watch from the camp as the man of her dreams turned away from her, convinced that there was no hope for her healing?

- *She left behind her favorite things.* What woman do you know who doesn't have treasured possessions? Different people have various collections that they cherish. For example, many women have a favorite dress or outfit—the one that everyone compliments because of its color and style. Did this woman with the issue of blood have one? As the years went by, do you think she had it thrown away? Based on her faith, I believe she would have told someone to fold and tuck it in the back of her dresser.

- *She left behind festivals and celebrations.* There were five main Jewish holidays where the families gathered for music, food, and fun. This woman would have listened to the laughter and the music from outside the city. Her memories of the "good old days," and maybe a plate of leftovers dropped off by a friend or family member would have been her only way of celebrating.

Stranger in the City

Of course, no one really knows what went on in this woman's life, but we know she was determined to return to something. In my mind's eye, I envision the woman awakening one day, as usual, in a pool of blood. But this day was different—something unusual was happening outside her window. She couldn't quite make out what it was. People were running and shouting. Finally she heard someone above the crowd say, "There's a stranger in the city and he's healing! He's healing the body and he's healing the sin-sick soul!"

The woman with the issue of blood got up as quickly as she could, cleaned herself up, and headed in the direction of the chaotic crowd. Her twelve years of bleeding had all but drained the life out of her—her steps were slow and halting.

I wonder. "Why was she walking alone? Where were her family and friends? Why didn't anyone carry her to Jesus?" But I knew the answer. Everyone was consumed by their own concerns. They didn't want to go through the trouble of being ritually purified after touching her. And besides, who would ever believe she could be healed, anyway?

As the woman continued to move toward the crowd she was walking on sand. The Scripture says Jesus was thronged by a crowd when he got out of the boat by the sea. It is difficult enough for a healthy person to walk through sand, let alone this poor woman who had virtually no strength left. I'm sure she was using every bit of energy she had to gain her healing. I saw her stop in the sand and consider what she was about to do. She knew it would cost her everything to push her way through that crowd. And what would happen if the people discovered they had been touched by an unclean woman? Wouldn't they turn on her in anger?

This woman, who had been hemorrhaging for twelve years, was walking in sand toward a crowd that had suddenly turned and headed in the opposite direction. You remember the Scriptures said that Jarius, the ruler of the synagogue, had asked Jesus to heal his daughter and that Jesus went with him

(Mark 5:22,23). The crowd followed Him, and the bleeding woman pressed in from behind.

The crowd probably wasn't kind. Can't you hear her saying in a weak voice, "Excuse me, sir, I must get through" or "Please ma'am, if I could only touch him." Apparently her courtesy didn't matter. By the time she reached Jesus, the crowd had either pushed her to her knees or thrown her on her face because when she reached out, she touched only the hem of His garment.

The moment she touched His garment it seems she stood up, because when Jesus acknowledged her healing she fell at His feet again. Then someone approached and announced that Jarius' daughter was dead. Jesus took three of His disciples and left with Jarius.

The Lord left the healed woman behind as a testimony of God's miracle-working power. I imagine her being lifted up in the air and carried back to the city on the shoulders of her delighted loved ones. She ran into her bedroom, pulled her favorite dress from the back of the drawer, and danced in the street long after the townspeople had fallen asleep!

The Real Issue

Whether we are male or female, young or old, most of us have an issue of blood. It is usually not physical; it's more likely mental and emotional. When someone hurts, disappoints, or defiles us, we begin to bleed. Even though physical blood is not being shed, the results are surprisingly the same as those in the woman's story.

When an offense takes place, we don't want the guilty person touching us or sitting with us. We definitely don't want them to lie down with us! We move outside of the City of Vulnerability into a camp with an encircling wall. Many times people don't even know we're bleeding. Daily we walk to the edge of the camp and talk across the wall in a courteous manner. However, if anyone comes into our camp and gets close enough to touch us emotionally, they also will become defiled (whether we want them to or not).

What about you? When did you begin to bleed and how long has it been going on? There are so many ways for us to be defiled. Most offenses happen during our childhood. Although some of the instances I cite may seem minor, they can have a profound impact on our lives and decisions. Wherever I've traveled around the world, people have confided in me that they suffered as children or teenagers who . . .

- were constantly compared with others, and never seemed to be quite as "good" as their brother, sister, or neighbor.

- had parent(s) who tried to make them improve through constant criticism.

- never got the chance to be children because they were too busy raising their immature parents. Mom and/or Dad lived a promiscuous life, was an alcoholic or addicted to drugs.

- were deserted by one or both parents. I have met many adopted people who love their adopted parents but, nonetheless, feel betrayed by their biological parents.

- felt stupid in school because a teacher was not sensitive to their needs. Maybe they weren't able to keep up. Perhaps they were teased by fellow students because they were too tall or short, thin or overweight, smart or slow.

- were betrayed by a boyfriend or girlfriend.

- suffered more serious offenses in the form of incest, molestation, and physical abuse.

All of these things can happen before we leave home! Once we get out on our own, we may experience betrayals in finances. Isn't it amazing that many times when we loan someone money, they not only don't pay us back, they also stop speaking to us? Or perhaps you thought you were marrying your best friend only to discover you were "sleeping with the enemy." I believe most people who are divorced suffer from an issue of blood.

Abortion has caused many women to bleed mentally and emotionally. They are haunted by thoughts of their unborn child. There are also instances of rape that cause women to flee to the camp and never want to return to the City of Vulnerability.

Some people feel betrayed by God. They can't understand how they could love the Lord, serve Him faithfully with their time and finances, only to find that He seems to turn His back as their marriages fail, businesses collapse, or loved ones die.

And last but not least (the list could go on and on), many people began to bleed in the church. Why? Usually because we drop our guard around God's people. We believe it shouldn't be the same way in the church as it is in the world. My pastor says, "The church is not a house full of perfect people, it is a hospital full of sin-sick souls; some of them getting better faster than others because they take their medicine." That medicine is the Word of God. In churches, we often see people putting God's Word in their mouths, but we can't be sure it's being ingested. They are not worshiping God, they are worshiping the Word and their ability to quote it to impress people with their knowledge. Those people can be dangerous if we trust in them because their focus isn't on God's will for their lives. Many people do suffer grave wounds in the church.

Counting the Cost

No matter what has caused you to bleed, the wonderful news is that you can be made whole. However, just like the woman with the issue of blood, you also will need to stop in the sands of time and realize it will probably cost you everything— every ounce of pride, anger, revenge, and bitterness. I'm sure you noticed in the story that there was a crowd surrounding

Jesus. There's a crowd surrounding Him today, too, which keeps you from Him. Your crowd is not the same as mine because different people have hurt you. But you will only be healed if you are willing to push through.

The first step is to allow the Holy Spirit to turn the first layer of the crowd around. The great part about looking into a crowd is you can't see everyone at the same time. Most of us couldn't handle that. But thanks be to God, He only makes us face the people who have hurt us a few at a time.

Who is blocking your ability to touch and fellowship with Jesus? Who is in the way? Haven't they taken enough from you already? Will you relinquish your fellowship with Jesus too? I think it's too precious to give up. As you look at the crowd you are facing, you'll have to make a decision: Will you press through or return to the camp? Some of the people blocking your way to Jesus may not be hospitable. You may very well find yourself on your knees or face reaching out to touch the hem of His garment. Are you prepared to make that kind of effort?

Jesus calls us to do three things in order to be whole, and they are equally difficult. These steps not only lead to healing, but they will help break the vicious cycle in our lives that causes us to attract the wrong type of people. Let's look at how Jesus handled people who had hurt him.

Step #1: He Forgave Us

Even while He was dying on the cross, Jesus pleaded, "Father, forgive them, for they do not know what they are doing" (Luke 23:24). The forgiveness of Jesus began with His disciples and went on to include the whole world. How many times have you recited the Lord's prayer, "Our Father which art in heaven . . . ?" Probably more times than you can count. We usually stop after saying, "For thine is the kingdom, and the power, and the glory, forever. Amen." However, in the next two verses, Matthew 6:14, 15 (KJV), Jesus teaches us a profound lesson in overcoming bitterness.

> For if ye forgive men their trespasses, your heavenly Father will also forgive you: But if ye forgive not men their trespasses, neither will your Father forgive your trespasses.

Jesus is speaking to believers, because He refers to God as "Our Father." He makes it clear that, even though we have the right to eternal life, if we have not forgiven someone, we continue to carry the weight of our own sins.

During a radio interview with a Christian psychologist and neurologist, the two professionals began to describe in detail some of the ailments afflicting patients who were bitter over their past. They said unresolved bitterness can cause a number of illnesses in the body: depression, anxiety, fear, high blood pressure, ulcers, migraines, back pain, some forms of cancer, and other stress-related diseases.

For the most part, forgiveness is giving up our right to judge people for their offenses, and releasing them from our own vindictiveness. God does the same for us on a daily basis. Has someone who betrayed you been living rent free in your mind for quite awhile? It's time to post an eviction notice.

People have said to me, "I have taken the step to forgive. But it seems like the feelings of bitterness keep coming back. What am I doing wrong?"

Step #2: He Reconciled Us to Himself

When we forgive someone of hurting us, we've taken only the first step toward healing. If we stop there, chances are that our feelings of bitterness and anger will reoccur. Hebrews 12:15 gives a clear warning: "See to it that no one misses the grace of God and that no bitter root grows up to cause trouble and defile many."

If there is any trace of bitterness left in our lives, it will rise up at the most inopportune time. I witnessed this first-hand in my marriage. Whenever something reminded me of my past pain, there was a definite response! In order to dry up the root of bitterness, we must take the next step in following Jesus. This step may be the most difficult and scary. It's called reconciliation.

Once again, we see Jesus teaching us about overcoming bitterness when we read in Matthew 5:23:

> Therefore, if you are offering your gift at the altar and there remember that your brother has something against you, leave your gift there in front of the altar. First go and be reconciled to your brother; then come and offer your gift.

Jesus gives very strong teaching about broken relationships. They are so important to Him that He is willing to send us away from the altar where we offer up sacrifices of praise and worship to Him. I have heard people say, "But I have forgiven the person that hurt me." However, Jesus makes it clear that *if someone has a problem with us*, we need to be reconciled with them. We need to first go to them—not call or write.

"But Bunny," some say, "what if I go and they don't receive me?"

That is exactly what happened to me. I went with a desire to see a family relationship healed. After four hours, I left crying. When I returned home after my attempt at reconciliation, I wept for three days. I didn't want to face Jesus. But one day He very gently reminded me, "If you love me, you will keep my commandments. . . ."

Of course I loved Jesus. But now was my opportunity to show Him if I loved Him completely. I asked Him, "What do you want me to do?"

His reply was simple, "I want you to call the person who betrayed you. From this day forward love that person unconditionally."

Step #3: He Loved Us Unconditionally

In my spirit, I heard Jesus say,

"Love your enemies, do good to them, and lend to
them without expecting to get anything back" (Luke
6:35).

My reply was, "But she is not my enemy. I understand
now that she wasn't a villain. She was a victim—which is why I
became a victim. And because I was a victim everyone around
me also became a victim."

I then realized that if the Lord expected me to love my
enemies, how much more should I love a victim?

If I wasn't willing to obey God's Word, I would be doomed
to live in the camp outside the city for the rest of my life. With
tear-swollen eyes I said, "Jesus, I want You more than my right
to be bitter. What do you want me to do?"

"I want you to call the person and tell her you love her,"
He replied.

I reached for the telephone and followed His instructions. As I replaced the phone on its receiver a weight lifted
from my heart. "Now," Jesus said, "I want you to begin loving
her unconditionally. I want you to replace any bad thoughts
with good and loving thoughts. If she needs something and you
are able, I want you to supply it. And I don't want you to look
for a call, card, thank you, or encouraging word in return; I
don't want you to expect anything."

I obeyed Jesus. For the next one-and-a-half years, I did
exactly as He instructed. Then one day, while having a conversation with this person, she said something that normally
would have sent me to the moon. My response was kind and
there was no pain. It was then that I understood the power of
unconditional love. *When you love someone without expecta-
tion, it breaks his or her power to hurt you. The only reason we're
hurt is because we have expectations.*

It would be wonderful if this admonition always ended
with "and they lived happily ever after." But we cannot control
another person's behavior. Thank God the Scripture didn't
read, "First go and be reconciled and *when* they have received

you, *then* you can offer up your gifts at the altar." Many of us would never be able to fellowship with Jesus again!

You can be delivered of bitterness while the other person in the scenario chooses to remain bitter forever. What is important is that you did what Jesus asked of you. In your obedience, you will be liberated.

Sands of Time

As you prepare to meet your Knight, it is imperative that you take these steps of healing first. If the spirits of anger, bitterness, revenge, self-pity, and fear have attached themselves to your life, you will inevitably attract a person with similar spiritual problems. Likewise, a godly man who has worked to be free of his past bondage will be turned off when he meets you.

Your Knight in Shining Armor will not be perfect. But he should be a man who has overcome or is overcoming past hurts that will hinder a warm and meaningful relationship with his future wife. You may be thinking, "Does a man like that exist?" The answer to that is yes, but you will never be attracted to him if you have not worked on overcoming the destructive forces in your own life. Even if you did meet him, would you invite him into your camp only to defile him? I hope not.

I know what it's like to press through a crowd that is trying to keep you from Jesus. There were times I wanted to turn back. Fortunately I didn't. I yearned to know Jesus in His fullness and to experience the abundant life He promised me. If I could go back and change anything, it would be to have pressed through the crowd before I got married. There were so many unkind words and actions that would not have happened if I had been a complete person on my wedding day.

You need to be *complete* before marriage so you can be *whole* in the marriage. You become complete when operating in God's fullness for your life. Marriage is the only symbol He has placed on earth that demonstrates the true nature of the relationship between God and His people.

You have the opportunity to make things right now. During your six months of sanctification, I pray you'll follow the direction of the Holy Spirit as he presses with you through the crowd. He will help you touch the hem of Jesus' garment. You will be healed.

—————— *Things to Think About and Do* ——————

1) Allow the Holy Spirit to identify the people who are keeping you from fellowshiping with Jesus.

2) Forgive, reconcile, and love unconditionally. If you are unsure how to handle your particular situation, you may find the answer in my book *Betrayal's Baby*, which has a chapter dedicated to answering questions on reconciliation.

Knight-Mare

How many marriage horror stories have you heard? You probably remember attending at least one beautiful wedding where a Christian couple gazed deeply into one another's eyes and recited marriage vows of unending love. You may also remember watching that relationship slowly deteriorate over the years, finally ending in divorce. It scared you, didn't it? If Christians can't stay together, who can? The big question you're probably asking yourself is, "Can I avoid the same thing happening to me?" The answer is yes!

One of the best ways to protect yourself from a disastrous marriage is to use caution in your dating life. Are you going out with the kind of man who would make a good candidate for a husband? If not, we need to find out why you're attracting the wrong type of individuals.

Daddy's Girl Forever

Let's go to the root of your relationships with males and start with your father. I once heard a woman say, "I am so thankful for the second and third person of the Trinity, Jesus and the Holy Spirit, because I could never relate to God as Father." She was speaking out of the pain that had been caused by her relationship with her earthly father.

Many women have heartbreaking memories in regard to their dads. Yet in my conversations with pastors and counselors, I've learned that nearly all agree that most women marry a man who is either:

1) just like her father;

2) unlike her father in actions but possessing the same spirit; or

3) fulfilling the role of a missing father.

As I reflect on the hours I've spent counseling both single and married women, I know that pattern is accurate. It even applies to the woman who has never met her father but is somehow aware of his characteristics.

"You Married Your Father!"

During a women's conference, a beautiful, petite woman named Debbie came to my room for personal counseling. She bitterly described her horrible marriage and divorce. Her husband had committed adultery, abandoned her, and married the "other" woman. She was left with a huge financial burden and the responsibility of raising two children alone. Following the infrequent occasions when her children spent time with their father, she would fly into a rage as they described his life with his new wife.

I asked about *her* father. She shook her head, "I don't remember my father. He left my mother for another woman, and my mother was very bitter."

I nodded. "It seems as if you married a man like your father." A look of horror came across her face. She couldn't believe I would say such a thing to her. Unfortunately, if Debbie doesn't take a serious look at how she's trying to select a future husband, there is a very good chance she will make the same mistake again.

Tuning into KGOD

It is fascinating to see how much the physical world parallels the spiritual realm. For example, our understanding of radio waves and how they are transmitted and received can help us visualize our relationships with people. We all have a tendency to draw certain types of people to ourselves and to repel others.

If you turn on a cordless portable radio, lift the antennae, and begin to move the dial, it will pick up every signal capable of reaching the unit. The listener selects the type of programming that suits his or her interest. Have you ever wondered how the voices and music get into the cordless radio? The simplistic answer is there is a radio tower that transmits a signal. The signal searches for a receiver. The receiver is located in the radio.

We know that Satan is the "prince of the air" and that Jesus is "King of kings and Lord of lords." So let's imagine that both of them are transmitting in your area where the stations' call letters start with "K." Some of Satan's stations would be KLST (lust), KFER (fear), KGRD (greed), KDPR (depression), and KPRD (pride). (Please don't confuse these fictitious names with actual radio stations in your area!)

Jesus only needs one station—KGOD. If we listen closely, we might hear, "This is KGOD broadcasting live from its heavenly shores. Now whatever you do—*don't touch that dial!*"

During your reconstruction process, I hope you'll be so tuned in to KGOD that every other station will be offensive. You can keep your dial in place by:

• Reading your Bible every day

• Praying for help and listening for answers

• Praising Him for His power and love

• Fellowshiping with other Christians

• Meditating upon Jesus' life and words

• Obeying His commandments

Changing Your Programming Format

Whenever you walk into a room full of people, you can be sure that everyone is tuned into some station(s). We are innately drawn to people who are on our frequency; we may even say we like someone because we are both on the same wave-length. The deepest parts of ourselves, our soul, our will, our character, will be affected by the kind of programming we've chosen.

Assuming you're a faithful KGOD listener, any man in the room who is single and truly loves the Lord and is working on personal wholeness will probably be drawn to you. However, if you're picking up KABS (abuse), KNGL (neglect), or KLIS (lies), you can also expect a man on those same frequencies to respond. Again and again, women attract addicts, victims, users, losers, and abusers who always have an excuse for their irresponsible behavior. If a woman transmits an advertisement that she's interested in rescuing lost men, you can be sure she'll find a few derelicts hanging around her door.

You didn't know it at the time, but as you were growing up your stations were being programmed. People were punching your buttons; your format was being established. Now it is up to you, with God's help, to reprogram your life. Once you lock onto KGOD, there needs to be a commitment to stay tuned into KGOD—I can promise you it will be difficult.

Intense static will be generated by storms in your life, but *don't touch that dial.*

There may.be times when high, almost insurmountable mountains cause the transmission to fade in and out, but *don't touch that dial.*

Other stations will bleed in and out, but *don't touch that dial.*

You'll go through some of life's tunnels, totally lose all reception, and be tempted to reach over and try to adjust the station, but *don't touch that dial.*

Don't do it! Wait until you break into the clear. You'll hear the sweet words, "This is KGOD broadcasting live from its heavenly shores. Stay tuned to 'Talk from the Heart' with none other than the Lord Jesus Christ. *Don't touch that dial!*"

Dear Old Dad

While we grow up, our earthly father is supposed to be a physical representation of our heavenly Father. He was instructed through God's Word:

> You shall love the LORD your God with all your heart, with all your soul, and with all your might. And these words which I command you today shall be in your heart; you shall teach them diligently to your children, and shall talk of them when you sit in your house, when you walk by the way, when you lie down, and when you rise up (Deuteronomy 6:5-7 NKJV).

> And you, fathers, do not provoke your children to wrath, but bring them up in the training and admonition of the Lord (Ephesians 6:4 NKJV).

When a father wanders away from God's instructions, it puts his children on the wrong frequency. Most likely he, too, was poorly programmed and passed those same preset stations onto his offspring. What type of programs did your father listen to? If he deserted you or he was deceased, how were you programmed by other people concerning your father?

By now you should be convinced that you need to retune your dial until you're listening to KGOD 24 hours a day. Unfortunately, many people have been cursed with undesirable broadcast formats from early childhood. It's wonderful to know that we have the power to hear God's liberating channel.

A Pocketful of Trouble

When Gloria was growing up, she idolized her father. He pulled himself up by "his own bootstraps" and was a successful businessman. She longed to spend time with him, but his career kept him away from home.

Gloria's father was an avid collector of expensive ballpoint pens. In the 1950's, it was a status symbol for a man to display those pens in his business suit's breast pocket. From childhood, Gloria connected those pens with success, and she connected success with rejection. After completing college and establishing herself in politics, she met Greg. He seemed like the perfect match for her.

What was perfect to Gloria? It was important that she marry a man who was a blue collar worker, like Greg. For years, she was content in their marriage. Then one day her husband began talking about finding a better life. He wanted to become a successful real estate agent. She had no problem with his goal, but she had a major problem when he achieved it.

How could she have known he would become so successful? Even after his first million dollars, she was miserable. But why? She barely noticed that he had started wearing ballpoint pens in the breast pocket of his suit.

One evening Greg called from work, explaining that he would be late because of a business meeting. He gave her all the details of where he would be and how he could be reached. When he returned home, Gloria was asleep. She awakened as he walked into the bedroom, and began raging and shouting. She screamed that he was rejecting her, and that he never had time for the children. Greg, who had made it a point not to put his work before his family, quietly responded, "Gloria, I am not the person you just described. Who are you talking to?"

In a flash, memories of her father began to flood Gloria's mind. She remembered the rejection, the loneliness, and the ballpoint pens. It all came together. Fortunately, Gloria was tuned to KGOD. She allowed the Lord to minister to her and to give her instructions about overcoming her past relationship with her father.

Much of how we think and feel was generated in our childhood. As with Gloria, many reminders stimulate our thoughts and decisions. Completely unaware, we are drawn to certain traits in people which have a direct tie to our upbringing. But much of it is hidden from our consciousness. Only the Holy Spirit is able to reveal those areas in our lives that need to be cleansed or changed.

Gloria had experienced rejection and loneliness in her childhood. That is difficult enough. But other women have confronted extreme situations which profoundly challenge their ability to become complete. Incest, molestation, rape, or physical abuse are cripplers. Nothing short of touching the hem of Jesus' garment will allow victims of these crimes to have meaningful marriage relationships.

Reprogramming

Edith's childhood was a tragedy, marred by disappointment and pain. And I was awestruck when I finally discovered all the terrible things that had happened to her. I couldn't believe she had lived through such horrifying experiences.

One of Edith's most outstanding features is the twinkle in her eye and the glow on her face. How can she be so joyful?

Edith overcame her past through forgiveness, reconciliation, and unconditional love. As she struggled to apply those godly principles to her life, the transmission signals from KHTR (hatred), KSFP (self-pity), KRVG (revenge), KANG (anger), and KDSC (discouragement) weakened. Her determination was to fix her dial on KGOD. She did so, and her life was completely reprogrammed.

Joyce, an attractive single woman in her early 40s, was also challenged as I shared my personal story and what God's Word says about forgiveness. She hung around after the service and shared some intimate facts about her childhood which had left her bitter toward her mother. After listening to Joyce's story, I understood why she felt justified about her feelings. Finally she cried out, "What am I supposed to do?"

Joyce was tuned to resentment, anger, bitterness, and judgment. I answered, "Since your mother lives too far for you to see her, you need to call and apologize."

"Me?" she shouted, "Why should I apologize? She's the one who hurt me!"

I replied, "You need to call to ask for forgiveness for your bitterness and judgment against her."

Joyce frowned and angrily retorted, "I'm not going to do that. I can't do that. It's not my fault."

"Well," I responded, "then you will continue to spend the rest of your life as an angry and bitter woman."

Joyce had never been married and wanted no children. Deserted by her father and hurt by her mother, there seemed to be no way she could receive the love sent through KGOD. She left me that evening, defiant and defensive.

The next day I saw her and she looked exhausted. She had been crying all night. When I approached her she said softly, "I did it."

Sitting down next to her I asked, "You did? What did she say?"

Joyce responded, "She told me she loved me and wanted to be friends. She just asked that I stop judging her for the things she did in the past."

That marked a new beginning for Joyce. She pursued the relationship with her mother, and chose to honor her, although there were times when everything inside of her wanted to pull back. KBIT (bitterness) no longer had a receiver. Joyce began to transmit forgiveness and love. A short time later she met her Knight in Shining Armor.

Before her father left her mother, Joyce had become very close to him. She had adored him. It was no surprise that her Knight possessed many of his good qualities. They committed themselves to in-depth premarital counseling for a year's time. Joyce is not only preparing for marriage, but has decided that she would like to have a family after all.

In chapter 1, you monitored your daily thoughts. Check back over your notes and identify the stations you may have been listening to. Were you tuned into KGOD? If not, make a concerted effort to reprogram your channels. The reprogramming begins with a decision and ends with planned determination. Proverbs 16:3 (NKJV) says, "Commit your works to the LORD, and your thoughts will be established."

It's wonderful to know that God gives you an opportunity to change the channel, no matter what your family has been listening to for generations. Are you tuned to KUFG (unforgiveness)? If so, the other channel that usually comes in just as strong is KJGM (judgment). Unfortunately, listening to those stations causes people to transmit KBTT (better than thou). The message of Matthew 7:2 bears repeating:

> In the same way you judge others, you will be judged, and with the measure you use, it will be measured to you.

One of the worst things we can do as believers is to pass judgment on another person. A guaranteed boomerang effect always brings our judgment right back to us. We may say, "I just don't understand why that person can't stop drinking." Yet if we examine our own lives, we can be sure we would find attitudes and behaviors that are difficult to change, too. It could be overeating, shopping, or talking. Maybe some people are saying about us as individuals, "I just don't understand why she can't stop. . . ."

On one occasion, I went out of my way to entertain a friend. Months passed and I never received a call or thank-you card. Fortunately, through hard experience, I have learned not to judge. Some years before, I would have thought, "I can't understand why this person doesn't contact me and share her gratitude." Instead, I said, "Lord, not hearing from her does not feel good. Have I done this to someone else?"

Immediately the names of five people came to mind that I had never bothered to thank for some kindness expressed. I responded by quickly mailing out thank-you cards. I'm learning not to judge, but it doesn't always come easily to me.

Are you angry about how critical your mother and father or some other person has been with you? The next question is, "With whom are you critical?" If we were to speak with your coworkers, children, and friends, would they all attest to your critical nature?

When we give up our right to judge the reason a person has committed a certain act, we release ourselves from being judged. At that point, we are reprogrammed with humility, kindness, and understanding.

"You Are Very Beautiful"

Janet was rocking back and forth on her knees with her face buried in her hands. She had come forward at a conference during an invitation. I had noticed her earlier; she was naturally beautiful but seemed to have an ominous cloud around her. As she poured her heart out concerning incest, rape, molestation, and many abortions, the Lord began His healing process. Toward the end of our time together, I said to her, "You are very beautiful."

Deep lines creased her forehead as she shook her head back and forth. She replied, "No, I'm not."

I asked her, "What words did your father use to describe you?"

Janet responded, "He said I was a dirty whore. And that everything bad that had ever happened to me was my own fault."

"I want you to repeat something after me," I gently prodded. "I want you to say, 'God says I'm beautiful.'"

Janet obediently recited the statement.

I then said, "If God says I'm beautiful, that means I'm beautiful."

As she repeated the second phrase, I could see her listening to herself. When she finished the sentence it was as if the sun had risen on her face. She started to laugh.

To God, all of us are beautiful.

God makes something and says, "It is good." When we begin to receive God's transmissions, communicated to the Holy Spirit within us, we learn to view ourselves from God's point of view. The message is very clear that no two people have the same voice-, hand-, or finger-print. A lot of thought went into each person God created. Dare we look down with disdain at His handiwork?

When you realize that you are exactly the way God designed you to be, and that you were not an afterthought, you will begin to appreciate your appearance and personality. No one can do what you do the way you do it. And as Ethel Waters once said, "God don't make no junk!" Stop receiving KLSI (low self-image); stay tuned to KGOD so the Lord can reveal to you the way He sees you.

Receivers and Transmitters

The messages we listen to don't end with us. We listen, and in turn we become transmitters. Whatever is in our hearts sends out a signal which is picked up by other people. The only way we can stop receiving Satan's transmissions is to become totally committed to the process of being complete in Christ. That is why I asked you to set aside six months for reconstruction. Let's go over the checklist. By now you should have:

- Started a six-month journal.

- Studied your thought life and begun memorizing Scriptures that will counteract any thoughts that would not please God.

- Allowed the Holy Spirit to identify to you people who have hurt you.

- Begun the process of forgiveness, reconciliation, and unconditional love.

If you are working on those key areas, your programming is being changed. That's our goal. However, through many conversations, I've come to realize that it is easier for people to forgive others than it is for them to forgive themselves. They stay tuned to KCND (condemnation).

"I Knew It Was Wrong"

While eating at my favorite restaurant with a dear friend, the topic of abortion came up. Candace announced that she'd had two abortions and had never regretted the decision. "I don't buy into this guilt thing," she said. "I didn't love the father and my career kept me too busy to have children."

As we continued with our meal, I asked, "Have you ever wanted to have children?"

Without pausing she responded, "Oh yes, but when I tried I wasn't able, so I figured it was just God's way of punishing me."

I hesitated, then remarked, "That's an interesting use of words. Why do you think He is punishing you? Usually when the word 'punished' is used, it acknowledges wrong doing."

Candace put her fork down and stared at me intently for quite a while. Tears welled in her eyes. Finally she whispered, "Because I knew it was wrong."

Until she was confronted, Candace had convinced herself that she had made the right decision, yet she knew, deep down, that it was wrong. Until a woman comes to grips with the act of abortion, it will continue to haunt her. And it will transmit guilt and shame.

No Condemnation in Jesus

Seventy-five women came forward at the end of a women's conference to acknowledge that they'd had one or more abortions. Several other women didn't feel strong enough to confess what they had done, including two who remained in their seats because their daughters were with them, and they didn't want them to know. As the women at the altar wept during that morning session, I offered them the good news that their babies were not dead. While in their womb, each baby was a living soul. Psalm 139:16 reads, "All the days ordained for me were written in your book before one of them came to be."

We know how Jesus feels about children, because He said, "Let the little children come to me" (Matthew 19:14).

I went on to explain that abortion is murder because it takes the life of another person. However, if we could see into heaven, I would not be surprised to see millions of aborted babies playing around the throne of God.

If you are reading this book, and you have had an abortion(s), you need to know that, in spite of that act, God will forgive you. He simply wants you to confess it as sin.

I believe that when women don't acknowledge abortion as sin, they subconsciously carry inner guilt which many times becomes Post Abortion Syndrome (PAS). PAS has side effects such as depression and suicidal feelings. There are even cases where it has led to murder. Some suffering women say they can hear a baby crying. And, like Candace, some hide their pain—even from themselves.

In Memory of the Unborn

Closing out the morning session with the women who had come forward to deal with their aborted babies, I handed out adhesive name tags. I announced to everyone, "During our free period, I would like you to write the name of your aborted baby on the name tag." Then I indicated where I wanted them to stick the tags at the front of the room.

"When we return this evening," I continued, "we will remember that your baby lives. Let's dignify his or her life by giving it a name. If you're not sure whether it was a girl or boy, you can give it two names separated by a slash. I'm going to leave some blank ones here on the table for those of you who didn't feel strong enough to come forward. You may pick one up during the break."

The evening service had already begun when I arrived. To my amazement, the front stage was covered with name tags. More women came forward at the end of the evening when we began the memorial service. During the break, the two women with their daughters both shared what they had done. The daughters forgave them, helped name the babies, and came to the altar with their mothers.

I read each name out loud. Some name tags had up to five babies listed. We sang, we cried, and we prayed. At the conclusion, I asked the women around the platform to stretch their arms out in front of them and then lift them high in the air. "Now," I said, "release your baby to God."

For the first time in many of those lives there was freedom. Since grief does not leave a family member immediately after a funeral service, I reminded them that they might continue to feel the weight of the loss for a while. However, there is a distinct difference between grief and guilt. In time, grief passes. Guilt is with us always. That evening they were released from guilt. If you have had an abortion, you may want to have a special memorial service of your own. Either share it with a close friend, or allow it to be private, just between you and God.

One day I hope that in every major city there will be a beautiful park with a tall granite stone in the middle called "The Tomb of the Unborn." On that stone will be engraved the names of aborted babies. It will be a place where mothers can emotionally and spiritually lay their child to rest, blessed with the awareness that God freely forgives everyone that asks.

No matter what caused your guilt, God wants to set you free. You no longer have to listen to KGLT (guilt) and KSHM (shame). KGOD broadcasts forgiveness and mercy. Are you tuned in?

Avoiding the Wrong Transmissions

It's worth repeating: Whatever is taking place in our inner being is transmitted to others. As we change, so do the signals, both coming and going. Don't be surprised when you start feeling connected to people who have been around you for years, yet you hardly noticed them. You will experience new freedom as you begin to drop your defenses. You may also find that some people aren't drawn to you quite the way they used to be.

Be encouraged! Those tragic endings to fairy-tale marriages don't have to happen to you. As you reprogram yourself to send and receive the message of God's love, peace, and joy, the Knight you attract will not lead you into a Knight-Mare. He, like you, will be growing in grace, willing to work hard on the difficult aspects of marriage, and ready to enjoy the many pleasures of a strong relationship.

Remember, if you meet someone whom you believe might be your Knight in Shining Armor, don't get carried away just yet. You are still under construction. Let him know your completion date. Your true Knight will be excited about what's taking place in your life. He'll also be grateful to God that his prayers are being answered. He's been waiting for a single woman who desires to be complete in Christ *before* marriage so you can be whole together . . . *forever after.*

_____ *Things to Think About and Do* _____

1) Make a list of stations to which you believe your father was tuned. Now, check off how many of those you currently listen to.

2) List past and present relationships with men. How many of those men were tuned into your father's favorite programming?

In the Heat
of the Knight

Have you ever met a single woman who didn't want to have a satisfying sexual experience with her future husband? I haven't met one. And yet, in all the years I've been involved in marriage counseling, I've come across very few couples who have reached that goal. All too often husbands and wives are frustrated by the lack of meaningful sex in their relationship. Why do so many marriages begin with high sexual expectations only to find their hopes dashed against the rocks of despair?

I can assure you, satisfying sex doesn't just happen.

Did I just hear an uproar from some women who are currently having sex outside of marriage, and thinking it is wonderful? The sex may appear to be good, but the reason is definitely bad. When you're involved in sex prior to marriage, Satan is in control. When you're making love after marriage, God is in the driver's seat and the only passengers He carries are those who are willing to pay the fare. The price? Discovering God's design for a healthy sexual relationship in marriage and working toward that goal.

Microwaves and Crockpots

While I was riding with a friend to an antique store, she announced, "I heard a Christian psychologist on the radio explain what takes place sexually between a husband and wife. I thought he hit the nail right on the head!"

I shifted in my seat and looked at her intently. "What did he say?"

She responded with a chuckle, "Well, he said that the husband is like a microwave—he just hits high all of a sudden. And the wife is like a crockpot—it's not that she won't hit high, it just takes her time to warm up!"

I pondered that statement as we continued to drive along and finally turned to her asking, "When you were single, were you a microwave or a crockpot?"

For a moment she looked at me with bewilderment and then broke into a wide grin stating, "I was definitely a microwave!"

I have spoken with countless single women. Some were sexually active and others were waiting patiently for their husbands before partaking in sex. But whether physical or mental, I have seldom met a single woman who is not sexually alive.

So how does a microwave become a crockpot? They don't look alike and they definitely don't have the same function. Although the results may be similar, they clearly get the job done in completely different ways.

I have often stated, "I believe God has called me to teach, to bind up the brokenhearted, and to set the microwaves free! If you're single, free to wait; if you're married, free to enjoy."

By the way, in marriage sometimes the wife is the microwave and the husband is the crockpot. Satan doesn't care which one is hot and which one is cold. His plan is to make sure we are not feeling the same way at the same time.

A Devilish Culprit

At an unmarried/married women's conference, during lunch I met the woman who was conducting the single's seminar. Over a steaming bowl of soup I questioned, "What did the single women want to talk about most?"

She replied, "During our question-and-answer period, most of them wanted to know how to keep from being involved in sex. What did you discuss?"

I couldn't help but smile. "I spent most of my time trying to get them to want it!"

Isn't it interesting? When most women are single they devote all kinds of energy trying to control their bodies and keep from having sex. Then they get married, in which God says sex is good and the marriage bed is undefiled. Yet one of the greatest challenges in marriage is sexual intimacy. Why?

Genesis 2:24 reads: "A man will leave his father and mother and be united to his wife, and they will become one flesh." The term "one flesh" represents the sexual relationship between a husband and wife. God created sex, and that means it is good. So why do single women seem more sexually alive than many married women? Once again it's our archenemy Satan. He's done a wonderful job.

Satan knows that a large percentage of a satisfying sex life is mental. The enemy is extremely accurate when aiming his fiery darts into our thought lives. For single women, it's as if he pipes continuous romantic music into their minds and floods them with thoughts of romantic encounters. Then, once a couple says "I do," when the marriage represents the physical representation of Christ's love for the church, the music falls silent. All too often, the couple's thoughts turn to disinterest rather than desire.

How can we stop listening to Satan's music when we're single? Once we're married, how can we start hearing God's symphony, with its melody of freedom and lyrics of commitment? It helps if we understand the Lord's plan for sex in the lives of His children.

Ripping a Beautiful Gift Apart

A distraught married woman came to my office one cold January morning. She sat across the table wringing her hands. After sharing her disappointing sexual experiences in marriage I asked, "Did you have sex before marriage?"

With tears pouring down her face she answered, "No! I wanted my husband to be the first. I really love him. I just don't understand why I can't reach a climax when we have sex. Both of us are miserable."

"Were you involved in petting before marriage?"

For the first time she smiled slightly and responded, "Oh yes. That's one of the reasons I am so disappointed in our sex life since we've been married. Our petting was wonderful."

I questioned, "Did it cause you to experience an orgasm?"

Once again her answer was, "Yes."

My next statement caught her off guard when I said, "That's the problem."

"What do you mean?"

"Did you think that once you consummated your marriage with intercourse you would be taken to a much higher level of pleasure?"

The young woman glanced at the floor and said, "Well, of course. Shouldn't it have been?"

Unfortunately, she and her fiancé didn't know that they were short-circuiting God's creation by jumping the gun and becoming involved in petting. They thought that by "playing around" they could relieve themselves of their sexual frustrations, and then, once they got married, the real fun would begin. They were wrong.

God's sexual gift to a husband and wife is a gift to be opened only after matrimony. Many couples have a tendency to rip off the bow, tear off the paper, remove the top, and peek inside at the contents before their marriage. Would you want someone to give you a gift that had already been unwrapped? It takes away some of the excitement and joy. Petting, masturbation, and pornography tear apart the gift box.

God's Spirit—A Real Person

A popular teaching among Christians states that masturbation is not the same as fornication because it only involves one person and no one is getting hurt. That's interesting, because God's Word teaches that every believer has a person living inside him or her—the Holy Spirit. Before I address the damage done by petting, let's turn our attention toward masturbation. Petting, for the most part, is simply mutual masturbation.

Let's take a look at that other person who lives inside us. If I were to ask you to describe the Holy Spirit, what would you say? Some people say, "He is an active force," or, "He is a thought," or "He's like a shining dove."

Most people struggle with the fact that the Holy Spirit is a person. And it's an important point, because the way you view Him is the way you'll treat Him. If you see Him as just a thought, a feeling, or an urge, it is easy to ignore Him. But if you believe He is a person who can hear, see, think, and feel, your response will be far different. The ability of a single person to hold his or her body in purity before marriage will be tremendously strengthened by an awareness of the Holy Spirit's presence.

Where does the Holy Spirit live? "He lives with you and will be *in* you" (John 14:17). And how long will He stay?

I will ask the Father, and he will give you another Counselor to be with you forever (John 14:16).

The following Scripture reveals some of the Holy Spirit's capabilities.

But when he, the Spirit of truth, comes, he will guide you into all truth. He will not speak on his own; he will speak only what he hears, and he will tell you what is yet to come (John 16:13).

In order to guide, He must be able to see. In order to speak, He must be able to think. And yes, He can also hear. Can the Holy Spirit feel? Yes. "And do not grieve the Holy Spirit of God" (Ephesians 4:30). The word *grief* is defined in the dictionary as exceeding sorrow. Have you ever grieved? It is painful and uncomfortable. If we have the ability to grieve the Holy Spirit, we can also bring Him joy. His grief is caused by our sin, His joy by our obedience to God's Word and will.

Some of you may be thinking, "It's so hard for me to grasp the reality of the Holy Spirit being a person because I don't know what He looks like." What does the Holy Spirit look like? "The Holy Spirit descended on him in bodily form *like* a dove. And a voice came from heaven: 'You are my Son, whom I love; with you I am well pleased'" (Luke 3:22).

Many people say they see the Holy Spirit as a dove. The Scripture says He descended "like a dove" but He was in bodily form. Unlike Jesus, there was no human flesh on the form. Then what does the Holy Spirit look like? When He is living inside us, He looks like you; He looks like me.

When people look into your eyes, they should be looking at the Spirit of God. When they hear your voice or feel your touch, it should be God through the Holy Spirit reaching out to them. The Holy Spirit is God and He lives within us. He should be a part of *everything* we say, think, and do.

Lovers of Themselves

Let's look at a Scripture which, among many things, could refer to masturbation. The Bible says: "There will be terrible times in the last days. People will be lovers of themselves... (2 Timothy 3:2).

You may have never looked at that Scripture in the light of masturbation, but this is one of the ways it is being manifested. It also means that men and women will be self-centered, self-absorbed, and self-controlling. In essence, men and women will be consumed with themselves and their need to be satisfied.

A woman does not just walk in the kitchen, get a drink of water, take it to the bedroom, and begin to masturbate. Her thoughts have to be turned toward sex. When a man goes to a sperm bank, he is given a pornographic magazine or shown a pornographic film. He becomes aroused, masturbates, and donates the sperm. When masturbation takes place, erotic thoughts come first.

Dwelling on sexual thoughts in your single life is sin. Notice I used the word "dwelling." We can't keep the thoughts from coming. Someone once said, "You can't stop a bird from flying over your head, but you can stop it from building a nest in your hair." Jesus taught that the sin of adultery not only took place physically but also mentally. Adultery is when a married man or woman dwells on having sex with someone outside the bonds of marriage. Matthew 5:28 reads: "But I tell you, that any who looks at a woman [or man] lustfully has already committed adultery with her [or him]. . . ."

Why is masturbation so destructive to a satisfying sex life once couples are married? Because it is self-gratifying, and no one knows our bodies as well as we do. A person who masturbates knows exactly how his or her body is stimulated, the right amount of pressure to be applied, and the thoughts that bring orgasm. When that person gets married there is no way another human being will know exactly what to do to satisfy him or her. And, if the person getting married assumes their partner should know or else doesn't understand how God's sexual principles work, even greater unfulfillment and frustration will follow. Many times these husbands and wives resort to masturbating even though they are married.

Pornographic Fantasies

Pornography also creates havoc because it causes viewers to focus on themselves—what stimulates, satisfies, and pleases them. Their concentration is on what *they* want the other person to look like, act like, and do for them. People who use pornography develop unrealistic expectations with regard to physical appearance, dress (or undress), actions, and attitudes. They are not dealing with real people, but with fantasies based on one-dimensional images. They become absorbed with those fantasies and with satisfying themselves. When the time comes, they are either unable or unwilling to give much thought to the satisfaction of a real-life, flesh-and-blood partner.

If you have been involved with masturbation or pornography, stop now and ask the Lord to forgive and heal you. Denounce those acts from your life. Commit your thought life to follow after Philippians 4:8 (NKJV):

> Whatever things are true, whatever things are noble, whatever things are just, whatever things are pure, whatever things are lovely, whatever things are of good report, if there is any virtue and if there is anything praiseworthy—meditate on these things.

God's View of Sex

Sex, as God intended it, is a celebration of His creation. It's to be done in His time, His way, and according to His will. It is an intimate, high level of communication.

I once heard a pastor say, "This is going to surprise you. God never intended sex to be pleasurable." I wasn't so much surprised that he said it. But I was very surprised he believed it!

Yes, sex was designed by God for procreation but *He made it pleasurable.* Based on the natural disobedience of man, I doubt that procreation would have ever taken place if it had been presented as a duty. But, according to Scripture, it was viewed, even in ancient times, as anything but an obligation! A quick review of the Bible book Song of Solomon gives us insight into a godly marriage relationship. How did Solomon's wife feel about him?

Let him kiss me with the kisses of his mouth—
    For your love is better than wine. . . .

A bundle of myrrh is my beloved to me,
    That lies all night between my breasts. . .

His head is like the finest gold;
    His locks are wavy,
    And black as a raven.

His eyes are like doves. . . .

His cheeks are like a bed of spices. .

His lips are lilies,

Dripping liquid myrrh

His hands are rods of gold. . . .

His body is carved ivory

Inlaid with sapphires

His legs are pillars of marble

Set on bases of fine gold. . . .

His mouth is most sweet,

Yes, he is altogether lovely.

This is my beloved,

And this is my friend. . . .

          —Song of Solomon 1:2,13, 5:11-16

King Solomon responds:

How fair and how pleasant you are,

O love, with your delights!

This stature of yours is like a palm tree,

And your breasts like its clusters.

I said, "I will go up to the palm tree,

I will take hold of its branches."

Let now your breasts be like clusters of the vine,

The fragrance of your breath like apples,

And the roof of your mouth like the best wine.

—Song of Solomon 7:6-9

Do you think it was boring in that bed chamber? Of course not. Once we've accepted the fact that it was God who created sex and that it is good, we can begin to understand why He designed it for marriage only. Becoming intimate prior to marriage is like picking fruit before it is ripe. Eventually it will make you sick (mentally, emotionally, and—especially now-adays—physically).

Having sex before marriage (fornication) is sinful. The same act within the bonds of marriage is honorable. The reason is simple: Once the couple has entered into a lifelong commitment through marriage, God sanctifies and makes the relationship holy. To God, a covenant relationship, like the one He has with us, is of the utmost importance.

"So, Bunny, if I don't get involved with petting or have sex before marriage, how can I be sure the man I marry will be able to satisfy me after marriage?" you might ask. Let me share my experience with you.

Finding the Right Combination

I wish I had been a virgin when I married my husband. I was unable to offer him that very precious gift—an unopened present.

Since I was robbed of the joy of sharing my virginity with my husband, I want the Lord to use my testimony to encourage women to sexually wait until after marriage. Even if you are not a virgin, you can commit your life today to live a pure life before God until marriage. Some people call this "secondary virginity." He will honor that commitment in your life, just as He did in mine.

When I met Frank, he insisted that we not have sex before marriage. Although he was not a virgin either, he explained that the Lord had told him I was to be his wife before we made love. So we waited until after marriage. Because I had had previous sexual experience in which I was not satisfied, I was able to judge the difference. Today our sexual relationship is wonderful, but God had to first teach me His plan for a fulfilling sexual experience.

For the first five years of our marriage, I was never sexually satisfied. I thought something was wrong with me so I did not discuss it, and Frank had no idea because I pretended. Was I trying to deceive him? No. I thought something was wrong with me and I didn't want him to suffer because of it.

As we were driving down the freeway one autumn day, I heard the Holy Spirit say to me, "Tell him."

I began a furious internal fight and responded, "Tell him? What difference would that make? It will only hurt him!"

Once again the Holy Spirit repeated, "Tell him."

Because I didn't want to grieve my best friend, the Holy Spirit, I turned to my husband and said, "Frank, I have something to tell you."

Frank looked at me and asked, "What is it?"

I began to cry and I cried for a long time. I can't imagine what was running through his mind. Finally I whispered, "I have never been sexually satisfied."

Frank could have responded in many ways. He could have shouted, "You deceived me! I'll never trust you again!" Instead, my Knight in Shining Armor responded, "What can I do to help?"

That began the process of my being fulfilled sexually. It didn't happen overnight. God had to teach me that sex is an act of discovery. Every person's body is like a combination lock. In order for another person to know the combination, we have to give it to them. If a woman or man is not sexually satisfied in marriage, it is usually because they never taught the other person what satisfies them. Or, it may be because the other person didn't want to learn.

I expected Frank to know my combination without being told. Other men enter into marriage believing they can satisfy their wives because of past sexual exploits. That is one of the greatest hindrances. God is fresh; He is new. There are no two snowflakes alike. We all have different finger-, foot-, and voice-prints. One side of our face is different than the other side. Do you think God would make any two bodies alike? That's the fun. That's the fascination.

The Delight of Discovery

You might be thinking, "But if I never had sex, how can I teach my husband what I like?"

Good question. On your first "night of discovery"—your honeymoon—begin by letting him know what feels good to you. Are you shy? Then play the hot and cold game. Certain ways he touches and kisses you may make you feel cold or warm or, best of all, hot! As time goes by, you will learn each other's bodies, and the fact that they constantly change. I believe boring sex is in opposition to the abundant life God promises. God is new every day and so are His creatures.

Maybe you're wondering, "Why do you have to be married to give someone your sexual combination? You know what feels good to you even before you get married. Even unbelievers can enjoy sex."

The only combination we can offer is that of our flesh. But God made us "a living soul." Sex not only involves the flesh, it involves the soul. Our soul is truly who we are—our innermost being, our thoughts, feelings, and emotions. Jesus is the lover of our soul and only He possesses that part of the combination. Do you think He gives it to just anyone? No. That combination is only given to those who have sanctified and set apart their sexual relationship through marriage.

Earlier in this chapter, I mentioned that sex was a very high form of communication that only takes place between a husband and wife. It allows them to be "naked and unashamed." When sex is engaged in properly it is a celebration of God's creation! Unlike pornography and masturbation, the focus is not selfish but is totally turned toward the other partner. The husband is to be consumed with pleasing his wife, and the wife her husband. In their total surrender to one another, they themselves become satisfied.

I once heard it taught that in order for a couple to have a satisfying sex life, they must think sexual thoughts about each other during the day. I'm just trying to figure out how we would fit that in. The Scripture says: "Blessed is the man . . . [whose] delight is in the law of the LORD, and on his law he meditates day and night" (Psalm 1:1,2).

It is not necessary to dwell on thoughts of sex throughout the day because each experience is a time of discovery. There is no way to know beforehand what will take place when it happens. What we enjoy sexually is always changing, and that is part of the excitement. Therefore, my daily thoughts are not of sex; they are of the Lord. And when the time arises, I know it will be totally fulfilling. Also, sexual thoughts throughout the day can lead to expectations in the bedroom. If those expectations are not met, we then have to deal with disappointment and frustration.

A missionary woman once told me, "I teach the teenage girls in my church how to abstain from sex."

"Really," I replied, "and how do you do that?"

She smiled as she walked along slowly, "Well, I teach them that sex is like a good meal. Before marriage you are really hungry, but after you say, 'I do,' and have your meal, you are satisfied for a long time. So I encourage them not to get too excited about it!"

Although I applaud this genuine woman of God's efforts to discourage premarital sex, I disagree with her premise. When it comes to marital sex, once in a while is not enough. I get hungry more often than that . And whenever I eat, I want the meal to be great—even when it's fast food!

I have counseled many married women who say they have a low sexual desire. They often say they are too tired and stressed. But most of those women love to shop. Even on a day when they are tired and stressed, if someone invites them to go to the mall, they come back completely refreshed. Why? Because they enjoy shopping. Until a married woman enjoys sex, there is no way for her to determine how often she desires it.

Of course there are women who have been molested, raped, or victims of incest. They may wonder if they will be able to respond sexually to their husband. Let me encourage you that there is a big difference between something which is taken and that which is given freely. Once you have touched the hem of Christ's garment, you can become one of those blessed women who have come through horrific events and still find sweet pleasure in the arms of your Knight in Shining Armor.

Four Strategic Questions

Speaking of your Knight, take time while you're getting acquainted to compile sexual information about your potential Knight. What are you looking for? Here are some questions to keep in mind.

Does he apply sexual pressure? Remember that you are looking for a man that doesn't want to break God's heart. If he applies sexual pressure while dating, you may become weak and fall into fornication—and that would indeed break God's heart. Beware of a man who stimulates you to sin.

If he doesn't assert sexual pressure is he godly? Not necessarily. It may mean he's bisexual (a life-threatening danger in light of AIDS) or that he actively masturbates. He may not feel the need to have sex with you. This is why single women must put emotions on the back burner while dating. If you keep your eyes open and allow God to show you the man's heart, He will reveal the man's hidden secrets.

Listen to your date's comments on sex closely. (Be careful—too many sexual conversations can lead to sexual encounters.) How does he feel about pornography? (Don't ask him about it with a frown on your face.) Give him the freedom to share his thoughts. Pay close attention to off-the-cuff comments. Is he preoccupied with sex? Does he avoid the subject altogether? If you're watching, God will show you.

Single parents, this is especially important when young children are involved. Too many stepchildren are molested, so pay close attention to his actions and listen carefully to people who knew him before you met.

Does he brag about his sexual conquests? If so, his priorities are probably not the same as yours. Furthermore, if he has a history of sexual exploits, you both may assume that he knows how to satisfy you! Since you have read this chapter, you know that assumption is foolish on his part. You are looking for a man who is willing to be taught and who will also teach you what satisfies him.

If he has been sexually active in the past, is he set free from his sexual obsession? Can he wait to enjoy a healthy relationship with his future wife? Get all the facts in your head before you allow a man into your heart.

Does he want you to tell him about your sexual past? If you are not a virgin, beware of a man who wants you to share in detail your past experiences. Years of counseling couples has convinced me that it is unwise and unnecessary to share that type of information. In the first place, it presents fertile ground for future arguments and accusations. It can also cause your future husband to compare himself with another man's sexual performance.

Has He Been Tested for AIDS?

Unfortunately we are living in a time where this has become a very relevant question. The statistics are staggering. Once you see the relationship headed in a serious direction, it is only fair that both of you come with a "clean bill of health." If it is clear that he has been sexually active in the past 15 years, he should be tested for AIDS and other sexually transmitted diseases. It is equally important for you to submit to testing based on your past sexual activity.

In Touch with Your Deepest Desires

By now, I am sure you are wondering what you are supposed to do with all your sexual feelings while you're still single. You may have very strong sexual desires, particularly at specific times during your monthly cycle. Of course, like every other behavior, the response to those sexual urges begins in your mind. And that brings us back to 2 Corinthians 10:5 that challenges us to "take captive every thought to make it obedient to Christ."

What have we learned about sex?

1) It is good.

2) It is a celebration of God's creation.

3) It is for marriage only.

Women, like men, often have very active sexual fantasy lives. Some women's thoughts may be overtly sexual—daydreams that involve taking an active part in sexual activities. Other women have a more subtle approach to their dreams—they imagine being held, kissed, and cuddled. Even though images of affection may fall short of X-rated mental material, they ultimately lead us to the sexual behavior. Dreams of affection can also lead to disappointment simply because some men are not particularly affectionate.

"Taking every thought captive to the obedience of Christ" means living in reality, not imagining what we'd like to be doing. It is essential for our peace of mind that we accept what God has given us in the "now." When we begin to create a fantasy world, we are playing God and not enjoying the many blessings He has given us today.

Dwelling on sexual thoughts before marriage, particularly the more explicit variety, is sin. Begin to call it sin when

Satan floods your mind with sexual images and ideas. Don't drift away into an imaginary world where you feel free to do whatever you want. Remind yourself that your mind belongs to God just as much as your body does, and that your body will eventually act out whatever your mind envisions. Instead of daydreaming, align yourself with God's Word. On this very important subject, my advice may seem cold and calculated, but these principles can save you from failure, disappointment, and even tragedy.

My next suggestion may seem challenging, too. I strongly advise you to be extremely careful about what you allow yourself to see in movies, TV, and videos. Do your best not to expose yourself to stimulating sights—and that includes soap operas (Uh-oh, do I hear some of you going through withdrawal symptoms already?). I warned you this six-month reconstruction process would be difficult!

There is no way to get around the fact that abstaining will cause you discomfort at times. However, I have a question for you. Which is more difficult: 1) Wanting to have sex and refusing? or 2) Having no desire to have sex and surrendering your body?

I hope you know that question 2 is more difficult than question 1. When a wife is not sexually aroused and her husband desires to have sex, according to 1 Corinthians 7:3,4 she is called upon to surrender her body. This also applies to her husband, when she has the desire and he doesn't. I can personally say that when sex is the farthest thing from my mind and my husband desires me, it can be excruciatingly difficult—unless I'm in line with God's will and His Word. When that happens, my body responds in obedience to God's desire for a marital sexual relationship. I do the obeying and God provides the feelings. The Lord has never failed me yet.

Last but not least, the best way to stop Satan from flooding your mind with sexual thoughts is a commitment to prayer. If the devil knows the result of his mental attacks will stimulate you to seek God and to intercede on behalf of others in prayer, his assaults in this area will cease. His goal is to get you to sin—not to glorify God.

Practicing obedience sexually in your single life will flow over into your marriage and will become a tremendous blessing. If that obedience is not developed, you will probably find that the rebellion that says yes in your single life when God says no will reverse itself; that same rebellion will say no to your husband sexually when God says yes. Fighting the battle to remain celibate in your single life means that you are getting prepared to have a wonderful sexual experience in your marriage.

_____ *Things to Think About and Do* _____

1) Consider what you were taught about sex when you were growing up. It might help to write in your journal what you learned.

2) If there was little teaching or if the teaching was negative, ask the Holy Spirit to change your thoughts and attitudes.

3) Commit yourself to celibacy until marriage.

6

Knight Life

Look around—sights and sounds of the pursuit are everywhere. Video dating services. "Women Seeking Men" and "Men Seeking Women" newspaper advertisements. Glamorous singles clubs, cruises, and classes. The psychic network offers hope for finding a "significant other." As the popular song says, "Everybody's looking for someone." Once a new love interest appears, the 1990s dating ritual begins with candlelight, soft music, and flattery. It usually ends in a steamy sexual seduction and, all too often, heartbreak.

Since we're not conforming to a non-Christian approach to relationships, we need to dispel some popular misconceptions about dating. What is the reason for dating? There are a number of answers to that question, but I believe that dating is primarily for collecting data. Of course roses, love songs, and candlelight dinners are thrilling, but the reason for your time together with a prospective husband must not become clouded over by a rose-colored romantic mist.

A Discreet Investigation

Do you remember your last job interview? Your potential employers wanted to know all about you so they could decide if you would fit into their working environment and expectations. We accept the fact that the process of hiring requires time and thought. Yet there are women who meet a new man, and without taking the time to investigate who and what he is, will stand at an altar and promise their undying love forevermore.

Since you're going to be with your future husband for the rest of your life, shouldn't your research be at least as thorough as a job interview would be? Does this mean you shine a bright light in his eyes and interrogate him with unflinching intensity? No. But it does mean that you begin with a methodical plan to acquire information—facts you'll need to make a wise decision.

Does He Make Wise Decisions?

In my book, *Liberated Through Submission* (Harvest House, 1990), chapter 4, "Submission and the Married Man," highlights your future husband's four main responsibilities. One of those responsibilities, according to Ephesians 5:22-24, is decision-making. Your husband has the right to make all final decisions in your marriage even though God will ultimately have the last word. If you are going to have to follow his decisions, what should you be studying while you're dating? That's right—his decision-making skills.

If the man you're dating calls to say he just got his paycheck and wants to fly you to an out-of-town metropolitan city and treat you to a dinner and play (Of course he would fly you back the same night because he respects your Christian walk and wouldn't want anyone to think poorly of you!), you would probably get excited. What a wonderfully impulsive thing to do! In actual fact, an offer like that should raise a red flag. It should cause you to become cautious about the man's financial decisions.

After spending a considerable amount of his paycheck on you, is he still able to pay his tithe, rent, car loan, and other obligations? If not, then you shouldn't be surprised when, after marriage, he takes his paycheck and impulsively catches a plane to see the Super Bowl!

In many of my marriage counseling sessions, the wife complains about her husband's shortcomings. When I ask if she saw any warning signs while they were dating, the answer is usually yes, but she really felt he would change. That kind of change seldom happens. When you see a red flag, it doesn't mean you stop everything. It simply means there are some speed bumps in the road, demanding that you move forward at a slower pace. A wise woman once said, "Don't marry for potential; what you want must already be there."

Attracting the Right Knight

Having applied the principles in the first five chapters, by now you should be attracting the sort of man who will be a blessing to you. Gone are the men who will be neglectful, abusive, jealous, petty, and unaffectionate. The reason, of course, is that you are no longer picking up inappropriate signals and your own transmissions have changed as well.

Usually when a single woman is attracted to a man, she goes into a "romantic stage." She gets butterflies in her stomach when she sees him, her thought-life becomes consumed with images of him, and she anxiously awaits their next meeting. A phrase from 1 Timothy that refers to elders adapts well as a single woman's motto: "Lay hands suddenly on no man..." (1 Timothy 5:22 KJV).

Another phrase that serves well as a single woman's motto is: "Patience is the weapon that forces deceit to reveal itself."

A single woman should short-circuit the romantic stage, and instead, adopt an interview mentality toward men. Remember Philippians 4:6:

> Do not be anxious about anything, but in everything, by prayer and petition, with thanksgiving, present your requests to God. And the peace of God, which transcends all understanding, will guard your hearts and your minds in Christ Jesus.

By keeping this safe-and-sane biblical attitude in her heart, a woman can walk in peace and security. She is able to drop her fearful guard and become open and vulnerable to meeting and enjoying all kinds of people.

A Modern-Day Love Story

The story of Teresa and Boyd (their real names) is a delightful example of proper Christian dating. Teresa was 25 years old when she met Boyd at her health club in Eugene, Oregon. The handsome young man kept approaching her and saying, "If you ever want to go out for a Coke or a bite to eat, let me know."

Since she had overheard some of Boyd's conversations with others, which conveyed a non-Christian lifestyle, Teresa knew she was not interested. However, she was always polite as she turned down his offers. During the next four months Boyd repeated his invitation many times.

"I don't mean to bother you, but perhaps you'd like to go out for a Coke or a bite to eat?" Boyd asked again. When Teresa politely refused, he became frustrated, put his exercise weights down and announced, "Fine! I'm out of here!"

Boyd stormed into the locker room and said, "Cold as ice!" A middle-aged gentlemen pulled his exercise shirt over his head and asked, "You think it's cold in here?"

Boyd answered, "No, I was talking about a woman out there who is as cold as ice."

The older gentlemen stepped into the gym area and looked around. There was only one female in the room—and she was his daughter. Teresa had already told her dad that Boyd kept asking her out.

"I hear you are a pretty cold lady," her dad said, chuckling a little. "Boyd just came stomping into the locker room and said you were 'cold as ice.'"

Teresa felt terrible about this and started wondering if she had been a good witness for Christ. The next day she was off work and made a point to go to the gym early to see Boyd. She found him lifting weights. "I hear you think I am pretty cold," she said very sincerely, meaning to apologize.

Boyd's face mirrored denial and he gave a nonchalant answer, "Where did you hear that?"

Teresa answered, "You told my dad in the locker room, and he told me."

Boyd walked away, flushed with embarrassment. He thought, *Now she'll never go out with me.*

Boyd finished his workout and returned to the locker room. Teresa quickly changed her clothes and met him in the parking lot. "Boyd," she said, "I really came here to apologize. I am not a cold person. And if you are free tonight, would you like to meet me for dinner?"

Boyd was amazed. "Really? Okay, I can meet you at 6."

A Word to the Wise

During dinner, Teresa explained why she couldn't go out with him. "I am a Christian," she began. "I am very active in Campus Life and I teach Sunday school in the high school class at my church. Jesus Christ is the most important person in my life."

Teresa went on to explain what it meant to be a Christian and how she was called not to be "unequally yoked." That meant she didn't feel free to date a non-Christian.

Boyd smiled and nodded his head as she spoke but didn't ask any questions. They parted and went their separate ways.

The next day one of Teresa's friends asked, "Do you think you'll ever go out with him again?"

"No," answered Teresa. "Besides, he'll never ask because he knows what my values are and they are different than his."

The following week, Boyd called her at work. Surprised that he called, she agreed to meet him after her soccer game. This time she brought along a tape by Steve Russo, an evangelist and professional drummer, in which he shared how he came to know the Lord. Boyd and Teresa sat in his car and listened to the tape. He asked a few questions this time.

Meanwhile, unbeknown to Teresa, Boyd's boss had been praying for the young man's salvation for two years. Boyd knew his boss was a Christian and said to him one day, "Teresa, this woman I'm interested in, says she can't go out with me because I'm not a Christian. What does that mean?" His employer opened the Bible and showed him.

Shortly after their last meeting, Teresa invited Boyd to church. She told him, "If you come to church, maybe we can go out to lunch afterward."

Boyd started asking more and more questions. He began studying the Bible at work during his breaks. At the gym one day, Teresa gave him the book *Classic Christianity—Life's Too Short to Miss the Real Thing* by Bob George. Inside the front cover she wrote Boyd a letter. She wanted to make sure Boyd didn't focus on the "don'ts" of Christianity and miss all the tremendous freedom believers share in Jesus Christ. He later told her that, as he read the book in his car, he broke down and cried.

Teresa saw Boyd for twenty minutes every day at the health club. They talked more and more, but it was always centered around the Bible. After church he would often go with Teresa and her family to lunch. One day her father said to her, "If there is a chance you are going to get interested in this guy, I want to spend some time with him. I think I'll ask him to go camping." Shortly thereafter, Teresa's father, her two brothers, and Boyd went backpacking. Teresa's father took the opportunity to talk to him about salvation. Boyd returned home giving Jesus serious consideration.

"You're the One for Me!"

Two months later Teresa was returning from an out-of-town trip. Because her flight was delayed, she ended up in Portland instead of Eugene (where Boyd was supposed to pick her up at the airport). She called Boyd from Portland and explained she would rent a car and drive to Eugene. He wouldn't hear of it. He drove two hours to Portland at 2 A.M. to pick her up. On the way home he said, "God told me that you are it. You're the one for me."

Teresa had heard that line before. She replied, "If that's true, why hasn't God told me?" She had seen Boyd grow in his faith, but hadn't really considered marrying such a new believer.

Boyd left it at that, but continued attending church. A few months later he went forward and received Christ as his personal Savior. A month later Boyd called Teresa's mother and father and asked if he could meet with them at the church. When they met he rambled on for two hours because he was so nervous. After Boyd left, Teresa's mother said, "Do you know what he was talking about?"

"I don't have a clue." Teresa's father shook his head.

Boyd had been trying to ask, "How do I show Teresa that I didn't come to Christ for her? How can I prove to her that I am doing this for God and myself?" Although his words never quite communicated his message, Teresa's parents sensed Boyd's sincerity. Shortly after that time, Boyd purchased an engagement ring and asked them for Teresa's hand in marriage. Her parents gave their approval because they had seen his life change. They also knew that Teresa would prayerfully consider his proposal and follow God's leading.

Meanwhile Teresa watched as Boyd pored over the Scriptures—reading his Bible at home, at work, and during breaks in his schedule. One day she called his boss, Bob

Adams, and said, "Bob, I just want to know if you think Boyd's commitment to the Lord is genuine."

"All I know, Teresa," Bob replied, "is that this man is not the same man I hired. He has made a 180 degree turn. Everybody is asking 'What happened to Boyd?' "

Teresa was leaving for Christmas to visit her extended family in Colorado Springs. December 18 was the date set to exchange Christmas presents with Boyd. As he drove her to an elegant restaurant, he seemed preoccupied. After dinner he suggested they drive to a lookout point in the city to see the Christmas lights. After parking the car he announced, "I want to give you your Christmas present now."

Boyd opened his car trunk and returned with two wine glasses which he filled with sparking apple cider. "Teresa," he said, "I love you and want to take care of you." Boyd reached over, opened the glove compartment, and pulled out the ring. "Will you marry me?" he asked.

Teresa told me later that she only had one thought: "This man has such a tender heart. He is the man for me and I'm not going to let him get away!"

A Woman's Sphere of Influence

God gives clear instructions on how He wants us to conduct our lives, and that includes dating. In 1·Corinthians 14:40 we read "Let *all* things be done decently and in order" (emphasis added).

Teresa's story provides a brilliant example of how exploring a potential relationship should be conducted. Even though Boyd was attractive and was pressing diligently to take Teresa on a date, she displayed an observant attitude. She wasn't so desperate for male attention that she couldn't think clearly. She listened closely to Boyd's conversations which indicated that he didn't have a personal relationship with the Lord Jesus Christ.

After her father mentioned Boyd's comments in the locker room, Teresa became aware that she might be missing a witnessing opportunity. It's perfectly all right for you to lower your guard and become open in conversations with men. God can use you in a tremendous way to plant seeds. Witnessing is sharing Christ in the power of the Holy Spirit, and leaving the results to God. Witnessing is *not* an excuse for dating a man you want for yourself—no matter what.

We women sometimes fail to recognize the tremendous influence the Lord has poured into our lives. Once married, a man has his sphere of authority but a woman continues to have her own sphere of influence. That attribute, however, is strongest *before* marriage. After marriage the woman is called to yield to her husband's final decisions and a great deal of her immediate leverage is lost. She still has power through prayer as she petitions God to speak to her husband, but we all know that God's timetable doesn't always coincide with our desires.

Why does a single woman have immediate leverage and strong influence over a man when she is dating? Because of the way God made men. Have you ever watched boys playing? Usually they are outside competing in sports and playing war games. Their purpose is conquest. Man's conquering spirit appears when he's in the hunt for a woman. He wants what he wants, and he'll move heaven and earth to get it. For that reason, he'll take the time to listen. He'll consider what you have to say. He'll try to please you.

Tell Him About Your First Love

When Teresa met Boyd for dinner the first time (she wisely didn't allow him to pick her up, which gave her the option of leaving at any time), her sole mission was to share with him who Jesus is and to explain that He was the most important person in her life. Her attitude was not condescending; she simply shared the story of her "first love" with Boyd. She explained that her relationship with God was the reason she would not consider dating an unbeliever. Notice that Boyd asked no questions which is why Teresa assumed he would never ask her out again.

Let's say Boyd did ask questions and gave the appearance of being genuinely interested. Should Teresa have continued to meet with him so she could teach him about Jesus? No. To have done so would have been a huge mistake—one which has been made by countless Christian females. Some people call it "missionary" dating. Many married women who come to counseling swear their husbands had a desire to know Christ before marriage. Those men attended church every Sunday, and some of them made professions of faith. Some were even baptized. However, once they said "I do," the religion game was up.

You can avoid that trap. Once you've shared your determined commitment to Jesus Christ, and the man indicates a desire to know more, tell him you'll have one of your Christian brothers contact him for further discussion. Whatever you do, don't be so emotionally needy that you compromise yourself and get emotionally involved with a non-Christian man.

Beware of Closet Christians

Let's say you tell a man about your commitment to your first love—Jesus Christ—and he tells you that he is also a Christian. Should that excite you? Only after you hear his testimony. You should ask him to share with you how he came to know the Lord. I have heard many different stories. Some people say they grew up in a Christian home and have always known Christ. We know that's not true. In order to receive salvation we have to realize that Christ was punished in our place—that He was the only one qualified because He was sinless—and satisfied. That is the real substance of salvation. Anything else should leave a question mark in your mind.

You may also hear, "Well, I believe in God and we have a close relationship but it is very personal and I prefer to keep it to myself." Remember Mark 16:15: "Go into all the world and preach the good news to all creation." When the Holy Spirit lives inside someone in His fullness, that individual is excited about the liberation that comes from serving the risen Savior. Beware of someone who has an "invisible" walk with the Lord.

What happens when you meet a man that is committed to the Lord, faithful in church, and knows the Scriptures well? Is that a green light? No, it's yellow. Proceed with caution. Remember that our goal is to be on the lookout for someone who "doesn't want to break God's heart." All of the marriage counseling we do is done with Christians, and many of them fit the above description. James 1:22 reads: "Do not merely listen to the word. . . . Do what it says."

There are people who can out-sing, out-quote, and out-teach the best of us, but if they are not practicing true Christianity in their lives they are like "a resounding gong or a clanging cymbal." If a man appears to be faithful and committed, ask the Lord to show you his heart. Be very observant during conversations he carries on with other people. Is he loyal to his pastor or does he complain about him and the church (this is in direct violation of the principle of submission)? What do people say about him? How is he viewed on his job? How does he conduct business if he is an entrepreneur? Are his professional decisions honest?

No matter how your first conversation ends, it is still just that—a conversation. Purpose in your heart not to become emotionally attached yet. There is still too much information that needs to be assessed. Be kind but cautious.

Interview—Not Intercourse

So what about the roses, romantic dinners, and soft candlelight? That should happen very close to the marriage. Most singles devote most of their time to romance *before* marriage and then fall into a humdrum existence afterward. That is backwards. Marriage should be the door to wonderful excitement, not a dead end.

It is very difficult to be objective when you are emotionally tied to a person. Once you believe you are "in love," you become blinded to any glaring shortcomings. And, judging from the soaring divorce rate, there can be a great price to pay. Now that you're committed to a six-month waiting period, for the first time in your life you should be able to enjoy meeting the opposite sex. Your goal is to interview—not have intercourse.

If a man does not know Christ and wants to date you, the guidelines are clear. He doesn't stand a chance until he has a personal relationship with the living God. No matter what his initial reaction may be, his conquering spirit will cause him to consider your words. Your testimony will either draw him near or drive him away. Jesus said in John 12:32: "But I, when I am lifted up . . . will draw all men to myself."

Single women have been given a tremendous influence to point men toward Jesus. When you capture that vision, being single will become fun. No longer do you have to put up a shield and spend time weeding out all the undesirables before they can have a conversation with you. Just assume that any man (the Holy Spirit will direct you if there is someone you should avoid) who wants to hold a conversation with you will quickly hear about Jesus Christ through your testimony. Make sure you don't hold on tightly to every available man for your own gratification. You don't have to formally date them to tell them about Jesus. You may even discover that some men you would normally discount are more interesting than you anticipated. By opening yourself to conversation, you may discover that your Knight in Shining Armor has arrived when you least expected to find him.

Careful, Thoughtful Dating

What happens after you meet with a man and he passes the first test? What is the next step? Don't let your imagination run away with you. It's important for you to keep your relationship at a friendship level. You have to be careful not to put yourself in a position that will give Satan any openings. Individual dating usually causes couples to become serious too quickly. And your weaknesses will become obvious, and may overwhelm you. You also face the unfortunate threat of date rape. One of the ways to ensure that position is to group date.

If you are only friends, going out with another couple (people you know) and meeting at a designated place allows you to retain the freedom to come and go at will.

Also, it is very wise to pay your own way. A man may view this as a feminist tactic, but your answer should put his heart at ease. Simply say, "I want to pay my own check because we're just friends. I'm sure that, just like me, you have bills and obligations to meet. The only man who can pay my check is one to whom I am engaged." Once again you have challenged his conquering spirit.

Some Important Red Flags

If you continue to have conversations with a particular man and you're both beginning to get interested, you'll need definite answers to some other specific questions (besides the sexual questions we posed in the last chapter). These concerns do not have to flow in any particular order. However, they need to be addressed. Remember, no one you meet will be perfect. Uncovering flaws does not mean you have to end the relationship, but it is a good reason to slow down and see if he's willing to change.

• *What is his relationship with his family?* This especially applies to his mother and father. If he has a terrible relationship with his mother, slow your developing friendship to a crawl. Notice I didn't say you had to stop; many people have had challenging relationships with their parents. However, a person who has totally surrendered his life to Christ shows the desire to take steps to right the wrongs.

If he says he doesn't want to talk about his past, hit the brakes! Don't forget we are a sum total of our past. He may share bitter feelings toward his mother and refuse to entertain thoughts of forgiveness, reconciliation, and unconditional love. That is the time for you to use your influence. Challenge him to follow God's Word in resolving the matter or to get counseling. Most men with angry feelings toward their mothers redirect their rage toward their girlfriends or wives.

Don't allow your friendship to proceed until he is committed to working through this healing issue.

If he has a problem with his father, it may have a direct result on how he will lead his home. As we noted before, when we sit in judgment of other people their characteristics attach themselves to us in some form. God has filled you with the spirit of reconciliation. Help him see the error of his ways through both your words and your example.

• *Is he accountable to anyone?* Who challenges him in his walk with Christ and the decisions he makes? One person is not enough. Hopefully, it begins with his pastor and then branches out to a few other spiritual brothers. There are three men in this country who I could call if I were experiencing difficulty in my marriage with Frank. Because of the respect he has for them, a call from them would cause him to address any unresolved problem we were facing. The reason it is so difficult for married women to get their husbands to go to counseling is because husbands usually aren't accountable to anyone.

• *Has he developed long, meaningful relationships with friends?* Be concerned about a man who only knows people for a short time. Also watch out for men who have no friends. Friendships that span years reveal a pattern of stability. Friendships also indicate give-and-take, and a lack of them may point toward a serious personality disorder. Also, beware of a man who only has women as friends. Why can't he get along with males? Watch out for any extremes.

• *Where does he attend church?* Are his church's teachings consistent with yours? If not, that's a red flag. I don't mean that differences can't be worked out, but doctrinal issues can cause problems. For example, if your man's pastor puts emphasis on spiritual gifts (speaking in tongues or healing) and your pastor believes that those gifts should not be in operation during this time in the world, that difference could cause future problems. If the man feels his pastor is right and yours is wrong, that disagreement could result in future conflict. However, if he thinks the body of Christ is made richer through diversity, that issue may not pose a problem. In any case, it should not be ignored!

• *Does he tithe?* Scripture is very clear concerning God's thinking on this financial subject. A man who violates this principle will experience a myriad of challenges in his life and many times will not understand why.

• *How well does he communicate?* Most of us never learned to communicate effectively. Webster's dictionary says communication is the art of giving and receiving information. If you give information and it is not received, you haven't communicated. Does he listen when you talk? Does he respond in conversation? I have heard women say they are fascinated by the "strong, silent type." Then they spend their entire married life trying to get him to say something. It is very important that your friend can express and receive ideas and feelings.

Dating—Decently and in Order

Teresa's father was a very valuable asset in her life. When he noticed her becoming interested in Boyd, he took the young man camping. Boyd, in turn, went to Teresa's father and mother when he was struggling to let her know his genuine feelings. Many women do not have that type of fatherly "covering" in their adult lives. If your father isn't available for that kind of protection, allow someone you respect to operate in that capacity—your pastor, a relative, or a long-time friend can serve effectively. It's important that the man you're interested in is accountable for his intentions toward you.

When I met Teresa she bubbled from head to toe as she talked about her husband. It was clear there was a tremendous amount of excitement and romance in her life. She handled herself "decently and in order" while dating, and now she is reaping the rewards.

There are rules to everything we do in life and dating is no exception. Spending time with a man should always begin with friendship—even if you secretly think it's "love at first sight." Don't be in a hurry. Guard your heart. Pray and watch.

Stop, look, and listen. The benefits you will reap through wise dating practices will protect you from more heartbreak than you can possibly imagine. Godly principles in dating can help provide you with an exciting, fulfilling future with your Knight in Shining Armor.

—————— *Things to Think About and Do* ——————

1) Rehearse your personal testimony—recounting how you came to know Christ in a sincere and precise way. Some women have a tendency to give every minute detail of the story, even if it takes hours. Try to reduce your message to ten minutes so you can hold a person's attention while sharing your important words about Jesus.

2) The next time a man approaches and initiates conversation, ask the Holy Spirit to direct the flow so you can find out if he has a personal relationship with Jesus Christ.

3) Make entries in your journal about how you see yourself changing concerning men. Are you noticing men you normally wouldn't be attracted to? Who and what caught your eye?

Knight-Knight

Most single women have unrealistic expectations about marriage. What about you—will your sweetest
dreams awaken to a wonderful marital relationship? I hope so,
but it won't happen by chance. You've got some work ahead
before you're ready to say, "I do."

Here's a fairly typical response to the question, What do
you expect from marriage? "I expect my husband to be loving
and understanding. I want him to encourage my talents. I
want to have someone to talk to after a long day, someone who
has a listening ear. And let's not forget—he's got to be sexy!"

Seldom have I heard, "I expect to make my husband the
object of my love and affection. I yearn to be there with a
listening ear when he comes home from work. I want to serve
him unselfishly, and I plan to surrender my body sexually even
when, initially, I don't have the desire."

Strange as they may sound, the second set of statements

reflects God's intentions for marriage. God is always more interested in what we give than what we get.

Is it any wonder many married women find themselves frustrated with a husband who comes home from work, goes straight to the TV or some other distraction and spends the rest of the evening immersed in his thoughts and pleasures? Much to his wife's surprise, his focus is not on extending himself to her needs. Instead he is consumed with his own desires.

Some of you may be thinking. "Wait a minute! Have I gone through all this work only to discover that marriage is going to be all giving and no receiving? I thought my Knight in Shining Armor was going to be a godly man. Doesn't the Lord want him to cherish me, serve me, and nurture me?"

The answer to that question is yes. And in some cases women do have husbands who serve, listen, and encourage. One of the most important attributes your prospective husband should demonstrate is a willingness to learn and change in order to meet your needs. However, in each of God's children there is a certain amount of self-centeredness. It appears in different ways but it's there.

One of the reasons I enjoy marriage is that it's a constant barometer measuring where I am in the Lord. When something arises in my marriage that makes me uncomfortable, I am forced to deal with it or pay the consequences. A single woman can lock the door, unplug the phone, pull down the window blinds, and stay inside until she feels better.

When a spouse is the source of discomfort there is no hiding place. Your spouse lives and sleeps with you. Some people think you can be out of sync with your mate and in sync with God. That's not true. When we are flowing in God's order, we have a heart to serve, sacrifice, and love unconditionally. That expression should be freely given first to our husband and then to others. If you don't "feel" like treating him that way, something is wrong.

Choosing to bring someone in your life as a spouse is a major decision. In Proverbs 14:4 we read: "Where no oxen are, the crib is clean: but much increase is by the strength of the ox." Literally, this means that when your barn has no oxen in it, it is always clean. You don't have to bring in food or water. And most important, there is no mess to shovel up! Likewise, if you don't have a husband, there is no need to cook unless you're hungry. There's no reason to keep yourself looking good if you don't feel like it. And you don't have to deal with the emotional, physical, or mental mess created by marriage. But if you get married, be prepared to feed and shovel on a daily basis. If you're not prepared to do that, it is an indication that your image of marriage is distorted.

Let's not forget, however, the last part of that Scripture. It says, "much increase is by the strength of the ox." Once again, in the real sense, the oxen is used to plow the land, plant the seed, and bring in the harvest. There is a real reward in having oxen. Usually our immediate thoughts go to the husband bringing in financial gain. But there is so much more to be reaped. He can also provide mental, emotional, and physical strength. A husband who "doesn't want to break God's heart" will strive to serve and please you. But it is not likely to happen overnight.

Frank and I celebrated our twenty-first anniversary in May 1994. It is amazing how we are still making new discoveries about each other. God made people so very complex that, like onions, there is layer upon layer of us, enfolding who we really are. As I look at our marriage, and at the marriages of those around me, I see three specific areas that contribute to godly marital happiness—submission, spirit, and service.

That Unpopular "S" Word

What word begins with the letter "S" and stirs up controversy whenever it is discussed? That word is submission. So weighty is the topic that I wrote an entire book entitled *Liberated Through Submission—The Ultimate Paradox* (Harvest House, 1990). Two of the chapters are devoted to submission and the single person. But I'll give you an overview now.

The most common statement made by a single woman when she hears I have written a book on submission is, "I don't know if I can get married because I don't know if I can submit." That proclamation indicates that she believes submission begins at the altar. However, submission starts early in life with parents, teachers, and other authority figures. It continues into adult life, and eventually extends into marriage. If it is not learned when you're single, there will be a tremendous price to pay once marriage takes place.

Submission is a very positive, powerful, and aggressive principle designed by God for every man and woman, whether single or married. It is positive because Jesus lived a totally submitted life and He is our primary role model. Jesus said that He always did what would please His father (John 8:29). Jesus was equal to God, yet while He was on earth He did only what the Father directed Him to do. His submission is powerful because it ushered in our salvation. In the garden of Gethsemane, Jesus pleaded with the Father three times, "My Father, if it is possible, may this cup be taken from me" (Matthew 26:39, 42, 44).

Jesus clearly expressed His desire not to be crucified on the cross. It was as if He were saying to the Father, "Isn't there some other way to get these people saved? This is going to hurt!" Nonetheless He went on to say, "Yet not as I will, but as you will" (Matthew 26:39).

If Jesus had not submitted to death on the cross, none of us would have the right to eternal life. Salvation is God's greatest gift to us, but submission would have to be the second greatest because it ushered in our salvation.

Submission is also aggressive. In order for us to apply it according to God's design, we have to aggressively stand against the world, the flesh, and the devil. All three attempt to force-feed us a definition of submission that says we will be subservient, inferior, and someone's doormat.

Webster's dictionary defines submission as "to yield." Biblically, it means to yield to people, precepts, and principles that have been placed in our lives by God. A simplistic definition is, "Submission means God intervenes." Whether we are single or married, male or female, during the course of our lives we are called to:

- submit to God (James 4:7)
- submit to our pastors (Hebrews 13:17)
- submit to our government (1 Peter 2:13)
- submit to our employers (1 Peter 2:18)
- submit to our husbands (Ephesians 5:22)

How does submission work? Let me use a broken traffic signal as an example. Before you drive your car to a destination, you probably don't pray: "Lord, whatever you do, please don't let there be a broken traffic signal at a busy intersection on the way to where I am going!"

Why don't we pray that prayer? Because we've learned through drivers' education or the driver's handbook that when we come to an intersection and the traffic signal is broken, the first thing we do is stop. We allow the cars on our right to proceed first. Then the cars on their right go, and continue this way until the traffic signal is repaired. Now, what if an order had not been established when we learned to drive? There would be utter chaos in the intersection, and people would be arguing and bumping into each other, trying to prove they have the right of way.

Have you ever wondered why we need the principle of submission? One possible explanation is that God knew He had created free-thinking individuals and by nature every person does what is right in his own eyes. He also knew that if any two people spent any amount of time together, sooner or later the communications would collapse—the "signal" would be broken. If an order had not been established there would be utter confusion in the relationship.

Unfortunately, there are many believers who do not understand the principle of submission, and their relationships are filled with anger and chaos. A judge once said,

"Ignorance of the law does not excuse us from the penalty of the law." Whether an unmarried person is male or female, he or she is required to submit to God, pastor, employer, and government. The level of submission in single life will directly affect the success of submission in married life.

Let's use your job as an example of how this principle is to be applied. Suppose your employer gives you an assignment that will take you away from the project you have been working on for three weeks. You feel strongly that his idea is a waste of time. Do you go to the lunchroom and complain to your colleagues about your boss's decision? If so, you run right into Philippians 2:14,15 which says:

> Do everything without complaining or arguing, so that you may become blameless and pure, children of God without fault in a crooked and depraved generation, in which you shine like stars in the universe.

According to that Scripture, there should never be a complaint or arguing done by a believer. Does that mean we are supposed to let people walk over us? No, the proper procedure works just like the broken traffic signal.

Should your boss make what you view as an unreasonable request, the first thing you should do is *stop*. You need time to collect your thoughts and keep yourself from reacting emotionally and saying and doing something foolish.

The next step is to *speak the truth*. You may be thinking, "Well, that won't be hard!" It will be harder than you think, if it's done according to Ephesians 4:15 where God's Word says we should "speak the truth in love." I was fired from my first three jobs because I aggressively spoke the truth in anger and frustration. God's love is unconditional—no strings attached. When you share the truth *in love* it means you will say exactly what you're thinking with the right tone of voice, facial expression, and gestures. If your employer does not agree with you, your next step will be to submit (yield) and give the issue to God.

Submission is such a powerful principle because it operates on faith and, "Without faith it is impossible to please God..." (Hebrews 11:6).

It takes faith to believe that God knows all, hears all, and will intervene on our behalf without any further input from us. It means we believe that He can communicate into the heart and mind of our employers (whether they are saved or unsaved) and is able to lead them in the right direction.

After Jesus died on the cross for our sins, God could have written, "If you confess with your mouth and believe in your heart that God has raised Him from the dead you shall be saved. . . . The End." God could have left us here to deal with life and the devil on our own, and just waited patiently until we died and went to heaven. The very fact He cares about everything we do is an incredible blessing. However, we have to allow Him to intervene to reap that particular blessing. This is worth memorizing:

Submission means
God intervenes.

When you get married, sharing the truth in love will allow God to use you as an effective "helper" in your husband's life (see Genesis 2:18). Many married women attempt to sweep controversial issues under the rug in the name of peace. That puts lumps in the carpet, and after a while neither spouse is able to walk through the relationship.

The last step is to *wait on God* to demonstrate what *His will* is concerning the situation. Notice I said *His will* and not who is right or wrong. Sometimes we can have all the facts correct, but the conclusion still is not His will.

It will utterly stagger the imagination of your employer as he or she watches you tackle a project you're directly opposed to with a cheerful heart and attitude. You've stopped, you've lovingly made your position clear and your boss knows his idea is against your will. Your pleasant behavior speaks volumes about your relationship with the Lord.

But what if your employer chooses to disobey God's leading? The real question is not "if," but "when." No one is perfect and mistakes are inevitable. However, when we operate according to the principle of submission, mistakes become blessings. Our faith says God can "hit a straight line with a crooked stick."

Mistakes are your opportunity to say, "Because I am a Christian I submit to your decision. I believe that God can lead a person in the way he should go. I also believe that if a person makes a mistake, God can fix it. Now what can I do to help?"

When Mary broke a bottle of expensive perfume and poured it over the feet of Jesus, His disciples were upset because they felt the money could have been used to help the poor. Jesus' response was: "Her many sins have been forgiven—for she loved much. But he who has been forgiven little loves little" (Luke 7:47). When people who are in authority in your life make a mistake, and you are there to help them fix it, that expression of kindness allows them to accept what they did as being wrong, instead of needing to justify or blame. It endears you to them because of your forgiveness. The testimony of Jesus Christ is clearly seen. The next time you give your opinion, you can be sure they will give it more consideration, because you will have earned the right to be heard.

Submission operates the same way in marriage. You should have received plenty of submission exercise with your pastor, employer, and government before marriage. You submit to the government by obeying the laws of the land. If the law says to drive 55 miles per hour, to fasten your seat belt and pay your taxes, you should submit. Are you ready for marriage? Just ask your pastor, your employer, and check your car speedometer when you drive. You'll find the answer.

A question often asked is, "As a single woman, am I called to submit to my boyfriend?" Scripturally the answer is no. God has not placed your boyfriend in an authoritative role. If you and your boyfriend disagree and you go along with his opinion, you have not submitted. You have esteemed him higher than yourself. You need to ask God for wisdom on when you should apply this principle.

Single mothers are concerned that their children can't be taught submission because there is no father in the home to model the concept. Submission is not a person, it is a spirit, an attitude. When you are having a disagreement with your employer, share it with your children and share the steps according to God's Word you are taking to fix it. Have them pray with you and tell them the results once God shows you His will. They will learn by watching how you conduct yourself with God, your pastor, your employer, and the government. When you get married, it will be easier for them to understand how the husband now has the role of authority in the home.

One day I walked in when my two teenage daughters, Launi and Fawn, were yelling at each other. I said softly, "You two need to learn how to resolve your disagreements the way your father and I resolve ours."

They looked at each other, smiled, and said, "Okay, let's do that." Launi sat down and looked at her sister and said, "The way I see this . . ." Fawn listened until she stopped talking and then asked, "Are you finished?" Launi nodded and Fawn continued, "Well, the way I see it . . . " In the middle of her sentence they both fell across the bed holding their sides while they rolled in laughter. As I walked out of the room the Lord said to me, "They may not be doing it now but they know what it looks like."

Are you allowing the principle of submission to work in your life? Do your children or friends see it by watching you? It's never too late to begin.

Have You Got the Right Spirit?

After you have checked your level of submission, you will want to do a diagnosis of your spirit. This time we're not talking about the Holy Spirit; we're concerned with your human spirit. In 1 Peter 3:1,2,4, we read,

> Wives, in the same way be submissive to your hus-
> bands so that, if any of them do not believe the word,
> they may be won over without words by the behavior
> of their wives, when they see the purity and reverence
> of your lives. . . . It should be that of your inner self,
> the unfading beauty of a gentle and quiet spirit, which
> is of great worth in God's sight.

God wants a married woman to possess a spirit that is meek and quiet. Oh, please, stop groaning—it's not ladylike. When most people think of meek and quiet it stimulates the same kind of images as the phrase "barefoot and pregnant." We'd better take a look at what it means to be meek. Jesus was lowly and meek. He was also a force to be reckoned with. In Matthew 5:5 Jesus said, "Blessed are the meek, for they will inherit the earth."

Our understanding of meekness tends to be somewhat different from God's interpretation. Meekness, according to the Bible, is *restrained power.* It means we have the ability to do something but choose to restrain ourselves. When the soldiers came to arrest Jesus, Peter drew his sword and cut off a servant's ear. Jesus said, "Do you think I cannot call on my Father, and he will at once put at my disposal more than twelve legions of angels?" (Matthew 26:53).

Jesus knew He was not helpless. It was within His power to wipe out all of humanity off the face of the earth. Yet He chose to allow men to hang Him on a cross. Of course He could afford to be meek because He knew that in three days He would rise from the dead. And that is exactly why *we* should choose to be meek. We know that things are not as bad as they seem. When people appear to be getting the upper hand, our assurance is found in Psalm 62:1-2,

> My soul finds rest in God alone;
> my salvation comes from him.
> He only is my rock and my salvation;
> he is my fortress,
> I will never be shaken.

No wonder Jesus says,

> Unless you change and become like little children, you will never enter the kingdom of heaven (Matthew 18:3).

My three-year-old, Gabrielle, has no concern for her safety. Even though she couldn't explain it if she tried, she knows she is protected. At any sign of difficulty she comes running to Frank or me for help. As a child, she teaches us a great lesson. We should be looking to God for our deliverance in every situation. We can afford to use restraint because we know we have a Father who cares about every single thing that takes place in our lives. If we will set aside our own solutions, retaliations, and vindications, He will respond.

Submission and meekness are sisters. Submission gives the challenge up to God and meekness waits for His answer. When you get married, there may be times when you are unhappy with a particular situation, and you know it's within your power to fix it. The solution will seem so simple. However, in order to execute your desire you would have to violate one of God's principles. When you refrain from doing so, you are exercising meekness.

There can be calm in the midst of the storm. When everything around you seems to be falling apart, there is an immovable quietness within that is not affected. It knows God has everything under control. Anxiety and frustration cannot live with a meek and quiet spirit. Depression and doubt flee. What is happening inside of you?

When you travel down your inner road, are the streets lined with peaceful meadows and flowing streams? Or are prickly tumbleweeds blowing across the road, carried along by winds of despair? We have the ability to choose the type of environment we live in, both inside and out.

Why does Scripture say that a gentle and quiet spirit is of great value to God? What makes something costly? The answer is rarity. The opposite of a gentle and quiet spirit is a loud and raging one. Keep in mind that these Scriptures are directed at Christian women. Unfortunately, married Christian women with a gentle and quiet spirit are few and far between.

A gentle and quiet spirit should be developing during your single life. What challenges face you today? You can choose to turn those difficulties completely over to God and speak peace to your spirit with the knowledge that God is in control. Let the Lord continue to show you that He will never leave you or forsake you (see Hebrews 13:5; Deuteronomy 31:6).

When you marry, certain events are going to cause you displeasure. Once again we see God's wisdom in giving women the "sphere of influence." A gentle and meek spirit challenges a husband from the inside where the real work needs to take place. It may not be obvious on the outside, but God is at work. If you practice this gentleness and meekness principle on your pastor and employer before your marriage, you will be in great shape for dealing with your husband after you marry.

A Servant's Heart

There is no better place to practice serving than in marriage. After all, shouldn't we want to serve the one person in our life who means the most to us? For many married women, the startling revelation is that they don't want to serve; they want to be served. And yet the basis of our Christian life is service. Jesus said,

> Whoever wants to become great among you must be your servant, and whoever wants to be first must be your slave—just as the Son of Man did not come to be served but to serve" (Mattew 20:26-28).

In this self-centered world the idea of serving seems foreign. But as believers, we understand that "Our citizenship is in Heaven" (Philippians 3:20). Ask God to give you a servant's heart and look for opportunities to practice a principle that will bless your marriage.

—————— *Things to Think About and Do* ——————

1) Document your next (or first) experience with submission. How did you do?

2) Pay close attention to your spirit the next time you are confronted with a challenging situation. Evaluate your response.

3) Look for ways to serve others, then practice serving them.

Knight Owl

Whenever I meet a sincere, single Christian man, I always ask, "What are you looking for in a wife?"

Although he may grapple with the second and third point on his list, the first response is immediate. The wording may vary but godly men always say, "I want a woman who genuinely loves God." Other qualities men often desire include intelligence, a good sense of humor, motivation, and kindness. Seldom are looks and age mentioned.

Recently Greg, a bright, good-looking young man confided, "I stay away from singles groups. It's disappointing to be around so many women who are using worldly ways to attract Christian men. You should hear all the manipulation and deceit that goes on."

A Timeless Love Story

There's an old Bible story about an available, wealthy, older single man who loved God. We find him in the book of

Ruth. He was open to marriage and surrounded by single women. His ultimate choice was a bride who seemed to be an unlikely candidate. Let's look together at the fascinating story of Ruth. Like the book of Esther, there are only a few short chapters; I hope you'll take the time to read the entire book of Ruth right now.

During the time of Ruth's story, there was no king in Bethlehem in Judah, and the land was experiencing a severe famine. A man named Elimelech decided to take his wife, Naomi, and his two sons to a foreign country called Moab, to get away from the famine's devastation. Once there, Elimelech died and the two sons married Moabite women named Ruth and Orpah. Then Naomi's two sons died, and the heartbroken woman decided to return to her hometown. She had heard that the Lord had blessed His people with food.

Naomi and her daughters-in-law began the journey. Along the way, she insisted that her daughters-in-law return to Moab, so they could find new husbands. Orpah and Ruth wouldn't hear of it. They wept and professed their undying love. Both begged Naomi not to send them back. But Naomi continued to paint a gloomy picture for them, and finally Orpah changed her mind and decided to return to her home-land.

Ruth had different priorities. In touching words, she proclaimed her undying love for Naomi.

> Don't urge me to leave you or to turn back from you.
> Where you go I will go, and where you stay I will stay.
> Your people will be my people and your God my God.
> Where you die I will die, and there I will be buried.
> May the Lord deal with me, be it ever so severely, if anything but death separates you and me (Ruth 1:16,17).

Ruth chose to sacrifice her pursuit of pleasure to serve her mother-in-law for the rest of her life. The Moabites worshiped a god called Chemosh. They were deeply devoted to this deity, and would offer human sacrifices to please it. This was the only form of worship Ruth had ever known, yet she was willing to make a commitment to serve a God she could not see or touch. She also made a decision to live in a country where she would be considered a heathen woman, where her chances for remarriage would be slim. Even in light of all this, Naomi sensed that Ruth could not be deterred so she allowed her to follow.

When Naomi entered Bethlehem the entire city came to see her. The story reads,

> When they arrived in Bethlehem, the whole town was stirred because of them, and the women exclaimed, "Can this be Naomi?"

> "Don't call me Naomi," she told them. "Call me Mara, because the Almighty has made my life very bitter. I went away full, but the LORD has brought me back empty."

An Overlooked Blessing?

In those days sons meant everything to families because they carried on the family name and received the ancestral inheritance. You can imagine how Ruth must have felt when Naomi didn't so much as even recognize her presence. She was so consumed by what she didn't have that she totally overlooked the blessing in her life. No wonder Naomi was bitter.

Naomi and Ruth set up their house and Ruth went out into the neighboring barley fields in search of food. She happened to go into a field belonging to Boaz who was related to Elimelech, Naomi's deceased husband. Boaz didn't recognize Ruth, and he asked his servants about her. He was informed that she was the woman who had accompanied Naomi from the country of Moab. Boaz called Ruth aside and told her to gather food only on his land; he ordered his servants to intentionally allow extra food to fall in her path. Naomi may have overlooked Ruth, but Boaz didn't. Ruth asked him about his kindness and he replied,

> "I've been told all about what you have done for your mother-in-law since the death of your husband—how you left your father and mother and your homeland and came to live with a people you did not know before. May the LORD repay you for what you have done. May you be richly rewarded by the LORD, the God of Israel, under whose wings you have come to take refuge."

A Plan for the Future

When Ruth returned home and Naomi saw the abundance of food she had gathered, she asked Ruth what field she had worked in. Ruth recounted the events of the day and Naomi was pleased. Ruth continued to gather food in Boaz's field, and one day Naomi suggested that Ruth become Boaz's wife. She gave Ruth explicit instructions about what she was to do and say. When Boaz understood Ruth's desire, he responded,

> "The LORD bless you, my daughter," he replied. "This kindness is greater than that which you showed earlier: You have not run after the younger men, whether rich or poor. And now, my daughter, don't be afraid. I will do for you all you ask. All my fellow townsmen know that you are a woman of noble character."

To make this short story shorter, Boaz married Ruth and she bore a son, who was to become an ancestor of both Israel's great King David and, eventually, God's only begotten son, Jesus. Naomi had a grandson to carry on the family name, and she became nurse and the mother-in-law of a very wealthy daughter-in-law.

It's clear from Boaz's response to Ruth that he had been observing her lifestyle. He knew what the whole city thought about her. Once again the man did the finding, while God was fashioning Ruth. Ruth was consumed with serving God and someone other than herself. Take note, however, that Ruth's knight was very conservative. His actions showed an interest, and Ruth was correct in responding verbally to his obvious intentions. Many people would have considered Ruth a fool, but God proved Himself to be faithful to His promises. Boaz was the perfect husband for Ruth, and he wanted her to be his wife because he admired her kindness, her faithfulness, and her humble spirit.

Is He Too Good to be True?

God-given love stories didn't stop happening after the Bible was written. Frank and I have seen God miraculously bring couples together time and time again. Every year, we host a conference for singles and married couples, at which a reception is held for first-time attendees. A couple of years ago, there were forty single women among the guests. As I looked out over the crowd, I tossed out an invitation.

"Frank and I know a gentleman in his mid-thirties," I explained. "He is part of our fellowship, a successful entrepreneur, and he wants to be married. If you are interested in meeting him, please come up to me after we're finished here, and I'll make sure you're introduced. He comes with our highest recommendation."

I waited to be swarmed with single women. How many responded? Not one! During a subsequent dinner, I approached a table with eight single women. One lady whispered in my ear, "Why don't you point him out?"

I retorted, "Why didn't any of you come up to me after the reception? Not one woman showed up!"

The answer was unanimous, "We thought he sounded too good to be true!"

By the way, before I am swarmed with letters concerning the whereabouts of that particular gentleman, allow me to inform you of his status. A year after I made that announcement, he became engaged to a wonderful woman. She was not

among those attending the conference. Although he was diligently searching for a wife, the Lord brought her to him from
3000 miles away through an introduction from a mutual
friend. Does that sound familiar? In chapter 1 we found that,
according to Scripture, the man does the searching and God
does the bringing.

Too many single women are sitting around waiting for a
mate who is holy, committed to Christ, financially secure, and
who will also be devoted to them. Yet when he is delivered to
them on a silver platter, the entree is passed up because they
are expecting a different kind of dish! That's what nearly
happened to Larry and Antoinette (their real names).

A Romance that Snowballed

He was 35 and she was 34. Neither one had ever been
married and they had no children. "We were married to our
ministries," said Larry, the youth leader in his church and a
businessman.

Antoinette was in high level management and also spoke
at Christian conferences. She had a special gift for teaching
teenagers. Larry had heard of her gift to speak and invited her
to conduct a seminar with his youth group. Although Larry
was open to marriage he was not actively seeking a mate. He
was confident the Lord would reveal his wife to him at the
proper time. When Antoinette arrived at the church, she sat
next to Larry before being introduced. As she was teaching,
one of the senior citizens in the church nudged him and
whispered, "She's single."

Larry enjoyed Antoinette's teaching but she didn't
appeal to him personally. After all, he was usually attracted to
tall women with long hair. Antoinette is 5'3" with short hair.
He also determined that she had no sense of humor, a quality
that was very important to him.

A year later, Larry invited Antoinette to speak at his
weekend youth conference in the mountains. She sat in front
of him on the bus trip and he filled her in on the agenda of the

upcoming conference. After she had spoken at a meeting the next morning, all the young people gathered outside. Larry decided he would fall backward and make an angel in the snow. When he stood up, a snowball hit him on the side of the head. He looked around to find the culprit and the teenagers pointed to Antoinette who was heartily laughing.

Larry thought, "She *does* have a sense of humor!"

Larry and Antoinette talked the entire bus trip home. "We spoke to each other every day after that time," shares Larry. "We knew after a few conversations we would spend the rest of our lives together."

Larry made an interesting point as he continued his story. "We decided to wait until after marriage to date. It was important that we not fall into sin. We met on March 5, and on the fifth of every month we would fast from 5 A.M. to 5 P.M. to guard against the flesh and to focus prayer on our relationship and marriage."

"How did Antoinette conduct herself before you were married?" I questioned.

Larry quickly answered, "She was very conscious about not giving an appearance of sin. She seldom came to my apartment, and when she did it was important to her that she leave at a decent hour."

"We made a decision not to put ourselves in compromising positions," Larry continued. "We wanted to save the romance for marriage. Sitting on sofas and watching TV at each other's homes was out of the question. It was too easy to start kissing and petting."

I asked Larry if the Lord had given him any special guidance about Antoinette.

"I felt that He was showing me that Antoinette was the woman I needed in my life. Even though I was physically attracted to another type of woman, the longer I am with her the more beautiful she becomes. After I accepted her as the person she is, my ideas about physical image no longer mattered."

"What were the qualities about Antoinette that stood out to you?" I asked.

"She is patient, caring, has a sense of humor, and is thoughtful," Larry responded.

I chose Larry and Antoinette as an example because of the tremendous love they now have for one another. Also, they are an excellent example of how God takes a couple from courtship to marriage. They married six months after their bus ride home. Their friends can clearly see the excitement and romance that continues to flourish between them since their marriage in 1990. Their marriage is fun.

"People would be amazed at Antoinette's sense of humor," Larry stated, "It's a side of her personality that few people see, and I am happy that she shares it so freely with me. That makes it even more special!"

Caring Enough to Be a Dad

Another couple met while they were in their 40s. He was single with no children; she was widowed with five children, ranging from nine years old to teenage. This would have seemed an unlikely union, but God impressed upon this gentleman the idea that she was to be his wife. After a godly courtship, the couple married and her children adored him so much that he adopted them. They wanted his last name. This couple has been married for over 15 years.

To the natural mind, it would seem that a single man in his 40s would not want to take on the responsibility of five children—particularly teenagers. However, when you put God in the plan, everything changes. This gentleman married a wonderful woman who has been a tremendous blessing in his life.

They Put Their Romance in Writing

Here's another story. Tony and Angela dated long distance. Tony was 37 and Angela was 41 when they met. He was divorced and she had never been married. Tony exhausted every effort to save his first marriage, but was unsuccessful. The challenges in the relationship stemmed from his wife's traumatic childhood. After his wife left him, he waited several years before deciding to pursue another relationship.

A mutual friend felt Angela would be a blessing in Tony's life and told him about her. Tony received counsel before contacting her, and it was suggested that their initial contact be by written letter and that they wait six weeks before their first telephone conversation. Because they lived in different cities, this would allow them to get to know each other in depth through written communication to see whether they wanted to proceed. Also, it would eliminate costly phone bills.

Tony submitted to the advice. He sent a letter and biographical information about himself. Angela responded in a similar way. Each letter ended with three questions they wanted to ask each other. At first the inquiries were about their favorite foods and colors. But soon the inquiries progressed to, "How do you communicate when you are disturbed?" "What are three things that irritate you?" and "What were the happiest and saddest moments of your childhood?"

With each letter the bonding grew deeper. You should have seen Tony when the six weeks was up! He was counting the minutes before he could place the call and hear Angela's voice! She came across the country to visit him shortly after their first telephone conversation. Arriving in town, she discovered there had been a mix-up about where she would be staying. Tony assured her she could stay at his home and he would go to his mother's house. Angela wouldn't hear of it. She said, "My witness in Christ is everything to me. Staying at your home would give an appearance of evil to your neighbors because you would be coming and going." When Angela opted to stay at a hotel, Tony knew God had sent him a woman who genuinely loved the Lord.

There is a different story for every age. The details change, but one thing remains the same: Every genuine man of

God who wants to marry is looking for a genuine woman of God.

What Does the Knight Owl See?

Like the wise old owl sitting in a tree continuously saying, "Who, who?" I wonder *who* is watching you? If you have caught the eye of a wonderful, potential husband, what would he see as he observed your life? Would you appear to be self-sacrificing or self-absorbed? In 1 Corinthians 7:32, Paul shares the purpose of the single life: "An unmarried man is concerned about the Lord's affairs—how he can please the Lord."

Paul felt it was better to be single than married, because when a person is married, his or her thoughts are focused on the spouse rather than God's call to service. But he also understood that everyone was not like him, so he encouraged some to marry, rather than to burn with sexual desire. In either case, the fact remains that the single life is an opportunity for the Lord to use you in His fullness. Of course, a single parent has to deal with her children, but raising sons and daughters with a godly heritage is serving the Lord.

Working to Serve or Be Served?

When you look at your daily schedule, what portion of it is devoted to God's service? "Well," some might say, "a person has to eat. Most of my time is spent earning a living. There is no one else who is going to do it for me."

That statement is true to a point. You can go to your job everyday, but if the purpose is solely to earn money, you have missed God's calling for your life. You can, however, go to the same job and ask God to use you to do His bidding, and in doing so, you are in service for the Lord. Does that mean you place a Bible on your desk and talk to people about Jesus all day? No! We owe it to our employers to give them a full day's work, and if there is any verbal witnessing going on it should be on our own time. Notice I said *verbal witnessing*. Ruth showed her love for the Lord by her actions. She selected her mother-in-law as the object of her sacrificial love. She practiced 1 Corinthians 13:4-8 everyday.

> Love is patient, love is kind. It does not envy, it does not boast, it is not proud. It is not rude, it is not self-seeking, it is not easily angered, it keeps no record of wrongs. Love does not delight in evil but rejoices with the truth. It aways protects, always trusts, always hopes, always perseveres. Love never fails.

On whom are you practicing this Scripture? Your parent(s) or relative(s), an employer, an elderly or physically impaired person, your children? Maybe you aren't practicing 1 Corinthians 13 at all? Perhaps you are only serving your own goals, agenda, and dreams? Does your Knight watch an unselfish woman or one consumed by anger, loneliness, and bitterness?

Your Knight may genuinely desire to be with you; yet from what he's seen, he may know that heartbreak would be inevitable. If he sees that your life is not yielded to God or hears you constantly recalling the past with bitterness, he could be very patiently waiting for you to change. It is unlikely that God would give him the freedom in his spirit to pursue you knowing your spiritual condition is weak. A man who doesn't want to break God's heart might be listening intently. What is God telling him about you?

Our Modern-Day Ruth

Are there any real-life Ruths running around today? Are any single women sacrificing their time and talents to unselfishly serve others? Of course there are. The stories are different and their length of service varies, but the self-sacrificing commitment is the same.

A Ruth came to stay in our home in October 1994. Christine is single, from New Zealand, and is twenty-five years old. Through a mutual friend, Christine heard of the various ministries in which my husband and I are involved. She volunteered to serve us for a year without pay, and to simply be available for whatever we needed. That could mean cleaning bathrooms one day or helping edit a book the next. By profession, Christine is a registered nurse. She could have been earning a healthy income at home, looking for the man of her dreams, and devoting her time to what she enjoys. However, she has chosen to make herself available to us.

A young man observing Christine would see an intelligent, gentle, committed woman. Although independent, she is submissive even when she doesn't agree, and she is yielded in her attitude. I am a better person because of knowing her. She has taught me what it means to serve and that knowledge has affected my thoughts and actions—particularly with regard to Frank.

This is her first time away from her family and she has braved the holidays without them. She brings me hot tea in the morning and checks to see if there is anything else she can do before I go to bed.

One day I turned to her and said, "Christine, I always knew God loved me but I never knew how much until He sent you to me." Only a single woman could share what Christine has freely given to us. It is mind-boggling that God cares so much about my overloaded schedule that He sent a person such as Christine.

Through Christine and others like her, I have developed a very personal appreciation for the freedom God gives single men and women to serve others. Are you investing your personal independence in God's economy? You may not be able to devote a year or more unselfishly serving someone, but surely you could find a few hours a week. If you have no children, have you thought of relieving a single parent or a married couple for a weekend? Is there an elderly person needing housecleaning or a ride to the doctor's office?

There is an endless list of needs in this world. When you feel compassion, get involved. Many times you don't have to look any further than your neighborhood or apartment complex. Be like Ruth, who was generous enough to put her own interests aside in order to love someone else. Serving others can be tremendously fulfilling. That kind of sacrifice will bless you. It will honor God. And it will prepare you to one day serve your Knight in Shining Armor.

_____ *Things to Think About and Do* _____

1) Study your schedule. Have you devoted it to God—to do His bidding? If not, are you willing to change?

2) List those areas where you feel a special sensitivity—for example, abused children, the elderly, homeless women and children, orphans, recovering alcoholics and drug addicts, or ex-convicts. Ask the Lord to reveal your area of compassion then ask, "What am I doing about it?"

   Let me encourage you that, no matter how small the amount of time you devote to your area of concern, you will begin to feel a sense of fulfillment unlike any you have ever experienced. Our sensitivities have been placed in our hearts by God.

3) List the way you would like your Knight in Shining Armor to perceive you. In what areas do you need to grow?

Knight Gown

Do you know what your wedding gown is going to look like when you marry your Knight in Shining Armor? One day I asked my thirteen-year-old if she had given any thought to her future wedding. After listening for thirty minutes to her explicit details of design and color, it was clear the only thing missing was the groom!

A significant amount of a woman's time is usually spent dreaming about "the wedding day" while too little thought is given to the seriousness of the marriage. Flowers, music, and a reception are all wonderful, but marriage takes preparation.

Marital Flight Simulators

My husband Frank will not marry a couple unless they have participated in 12 or more weeks of premarital counseling. He knows that the chances of a marriage surviving is greatly increased when the proper information is received *before* marriage.

During Desert Storm most of the pilots involved in aviation dog fights had never been in a real confrontation with an enemy jet. Yet the American airborne forces were outstanding. Why did they do so well? They spent countless hours in simulators. A simulator visually creates a real-life situation. If the pilots made a mistake, the simulator would indicate they had been hit.

Premarital counseling amounts to much the same thing. Couples can avoid entering marriage unadvisedly or lightly by enrolling themselves in a program that prepares them for marriage. Many issues come up after the wedding that weren't discussed while dating. There are five major reasons for marital breakdown. They are:

- communication

- finances

- sex

- in-laws and friends

- spiritual immaturity

During premarital counseling, real-life examples are depicted in these areas, and engaged couples work through various challenges. This allows each of them to see how the other thinks. Very seldom does balancing the checkbook, disciplining the children, or dealing with a mother-in-law come up in conversation between a dating couple, yet those are the kinds of issues that cause major conflicts.

Premarital counseling is not a setting in which couples put on rose-colored glasses, and it doesn't permit potential brides and grooms to ignore obvious problems caused by different points of view. I know of two occasions where couples decided they should not get married after finishing their counseling. It was the wisest decision they could have made, saving years of heartache and pain when compared to the short-lived anguish of a broken engagement.

A Test Case

Since in-laws can be a source of trouble in marriage, one of our premarital counseling examples deals with a mother-in-law. Suppose "Fred's" mother is visiting for a month. She has a heart condition and has asked Fred and Martha to keep their bedroom door open at night in case she needs help. What would you do?

The answer from the man usually depends on how he feels about his mother. If the mother and son are very close, he usually doesn't see anything wrong with the suggestion. In marital counseling he is taught that when he gets married he promises to "leave his father and mother and be united to his wife" (Genesis 2:24). An open bedroom door will affect the sex life of the couple and thus be in violation of God's Word.

One solution is to purchase a monitoring system (like the ones used for babies) so the couple can hear what is going on in the mother's room without her hearing them. If his mother still insists that the door be kept open, it will be up to Fred to be firm and explain that it is not possible. In the counseling session, if the man says he is unwilling to make that decision (or something comparable) concerning his mother, then the fiancé needs to hit the marriage brakes. Otherwise, there will probably be considerable trouble in the future concerning Fred's mother.

Considering the Vow

The central purpose of the wedding ceremony is the reciting of the vows. A solemn commitment is made to God and to each other in the presence of witnesses that can testify that they heard you speak your commitment aloud.

How does God feel about human vows? In Ecclesiastes 5:4,5 He says,

When you make a vow to God, do not delay in fulfilling it. He has no pleasure in fools; fulfill your vow. It is
better not to vow than to vow and not fulfill it. Do not
let your mouth lead you into sin. And do not protest to
the temple messenger, "My vow was a mistake."

The wedding vow is taken by two people to formalize a
lifelong commitment. Each couple is held accountable for the
promises they make to each other. After studying this next
section you may decide that marriage is too great a commitment. Let's look at the wedding ceremony.

The minister usually begins with, "Dearly beloved, we
are gathered together here in the sight of God and in the face of
this company. . . ." The vow-making ceremony begins with
God, the couple, and the witnesses.

The minister continues, "It is not to be entered into
unadvisedly or lightly." By the time the marriage takes place,
the couple should have received sound premarital counseling.

He goes on, stating that the marriage should be entered
into "reverently, discreetly, advisedly, soberly and in the fear
of God. Into this holy estate these two persons present come
now to be joined." Webster's dictionary says *reverence* means
"extravagant respect or admiration for an object of esteem."
To stand at an altar with your future husband pays honor to
God for creating the institution of marriage. It also recognizes
what God intended for that institution. Wouldn't you agree
that it would be ludicrous for you to tell me you have a deep
respect and admiration for the books I have written when
you've never read them? Unfortunately, many couples recite
their vows and don't have a clue as to what God's intentions
are for their union.

The dictionary defines the word *discreetly* as "having or
showing discernment or good judgment in conduct and
speech" and *soberly* as "unhurried and calm." To simplify the
commitment would be to say, "I did not rush into this relationship. I took my time, received sound counsel, and thoughtfully
considered the vow I am making to God in the presence of
witnesses."

The next part states the couple's commitment. Please take your time as you read this section. Consider the vow carefully. Since you're a woman, we will study your part. The minister says "I (your name) take thee (your fiancé's name) to have and to hold from this day forward, *for better for worse, for richer for poorer, in sickness and in health, to love and to cherish, till death us do part,* according to God's holy ordinance; and thereto I plight (give) thee my troth (pledge)."

From Bad to Worse

If couples kept this promise, divorce would become almost nonexistent. The promise to God is not to keep that person in your life if they are good or bad but goes one step further to "better or worse." What English phrase is more extreme than "better or worse"? Those words represent the ultimate. No matter how good or how bad, you are promising to remain committed to that person. Keep in mind that no one is forcing you to make this vow. That is why God holds you accountable.

You might be thinking, "But what if he physically abuses me?" According to the vow, you can leave the behavior but not the person. Counselors recommend that the first time a spouse is abused she (or he) should find a safe house (not a relative's home which sometimes leads to domestic violence with family members). She should contact the husband and let him know that only when he has completed counseling and it is safe to return home will she come back. This is called tough love. The purpose is to force the husband to get help. This is a "worse" case scenario.

You might ask, "What if it's verbal abuse?" As emotionally painful as that experience can be, God has equipped us to handle verbal abuse. It's not easy, and it can take years, but the Lord's instructions are clear when He says:

You have heard that it was said, "Eye for eye, and tooth for tooth." But I tell you, Do not resist an evil person (Matthew 5:38,39).

A gentle answer turns away wrath (Proverbs 15:1).

God expects us to continuously turn the other cheek when we are verbally abused. Our kind actions are compared in Scripture to pouring hot coals of fire on the head of our enemy. Is it easy? No. Is it commanded? Yes. That is one reason why it is so important to watch a person's communication patterns while dating.

A woman once said to me, "He didn't start speaking unkindly until after we were married."

"How did he speak to his relatives and coworkers before marriage?" I asked.

She replied, "He was often abrupt and cutting. But I didn't think he would do that with me." Always remember— whatever a person consistently does to others, he will eventually do to you.

Weighing the Extremes

Terrible situations sometimes take place in marriages. Someone might say to you, "John is an alcoholic."

"That's bad," you say.

"He's not only an alcoholic, he also gambles," they say. You say, "That's worse."

Things can be bad—very bad. But the vow says you will stay committed through the worst. That is why it is so important to select a man with good character—someone who comes highly recommended by several people. People are creatures of habit and will continue to do what they have always done. If a person's life has been changed by a personal encounter with Jesus Christ, a consistent, altered pattern should be evident. Never marry a man who has a past filled with abuses and dysfunctions soon after he has received the Lord. It will take a while to see if his commitment to Christ is sincere, and he may need several years to break bad habits and develop new ones.

Jerry was out joy-riding with some of his friends when the police pulled them over. Little did he know that the trunk of the car was full of cocaine. He was convicted and sent to prison for a year. He received letters faithfully from his friend, Amy. They were schoolmates, but there was no romance involved. When he got ready to leave the prison, his cellmate, Ron, asked if he would ask Amy to write to him.

Amy saw no harm in writing to Ron, and they struck up a letter relationship. Warmth and thoughtfulness flowed from Ron's letters. He wrote that he was a changed man. Ron and Amy were married on the day he was released from prison— two years after they began their correspondence. Tragically, Ron was sent back to prison a year later for attempted murder. Can you guess the victim? That's right, it was Amy. The promise was for better or worse, and her situation was extremely worse.

To a far lesser degree, "worse" can simply involve the changes that come from the passing of time. It can mean unpleasant things like baldness, dentures or missing teeth, weight gain or loss, bifocals, special diets, or sexual dysfunction. Without exception, "worse" will involve loss of youth and diminishing physical beauty. Those kinds of changes are inevitable.

The vow also says, for "richer or poorer." No matter how rich or how poor, you are promising to always stay with the person you are marrying. So many marriages fail because of finances! It is imperative to watch how your prospective mate handles money. Does he have a track record of keeping a job and paying his bills? What does he want to do with his life?

If you begin to make more money than he does, will your attitude toward him change because he is "poorer"? His attitude toward you could become defensive, jealous, or resentful because you're "richer." What if he decides "since you're doing so well," he will retire at 35 and let you support him?

How well do you know the man you're marrying?

What Kind of Sickness?

It seems the only part of the marriage vow that is still intact today is "in sickness and health." If the entire vow were taken as seriously as this part, there would be very few divorces.

Brenda shook her head in disgust. "I don't love my husband. We haven't slept together in months. I'm bringing in most of the money, making most of the decisions, and I want out!"

I asked, "If your husband were in a car accident tonight, and he became a paraplegic, would you leave him?"

Without hesitation she said, "Of course not!"

"Why?"

Brenda replied, "Because he couldn't help himself and people would think I was a terrible person."

"But you wouldn't be able to sleep together, he'd be bringing in no money, and you would have to make all the decisions."

"I know," she said, "but that would be different."

Many people would say that Brenda is right. There is an unspoken law stating that a good wife would never leave a sick husband, and vice versa. In this situation relatives and friends will gather around to encourage you not to forsake your mate in his time of need. No matter how severe the pressure and hardship, your self-sacrificing commitment will be expected. However, those same relatives and friends might be the first to suggest you leave your marriage if your spouse is not bringing in enough money or if there is a communication, in-law, or sexual problem.

When there is physical illness you can usually see the person's need. But if the challenge is mental and emotional, the problem is invisible. I have met men who are emotionally paraplegic. They can't respond warmly and affectionately— somehow their childhood made sure of that. When you can't touch the wheelchair or see the crutches, the level of sympathy and compassion is not the same.

In the wedding vow there is no definition of "sickness." The commitment rests on 1 Corinthians 13:7,8 where love "bears all things, believes all things, hopes all things, endures all things. Love never fails. . . ."

Love, Honor, and Obey

In the wedding ceremony the minister asks, "Will you have this man to be thy wedded husband, to live together after God's ordinance in the holy estate of matrimony? Will you love, honor, and obey, and keep him in sickness and in health; and forsaking all others, keep thee only unto him, as long as you both shall live?"

The word "obey" means to live in submission to your husband. I hope I have your attention! When you repeat this part of the vow you *are promising God that your husband will have the right to make all final decisions regarding your life from now on.* To marry a man who is not listening clearly to God is to put your life in serious jeopardy of spinning out of control. Yet, because you've promised to be with him for better or worse, you can't (shouldn't) get off the merry-go-round.

What is your profession or ministry? Your husband will have the right to say, "I don't think you should be doing that anymore." Think about it. Serious consideration of these issues will cause you to be very circumspect about who you marry.

Janet is a trained dancer. A year after her marriage to Carl, she shared with him her vision of praise dancing in the church—the Lord had shown her just how He wanted it done. Carl vetoed the idea. Janet submitted to her husband's will, but she also continued to practice her dance. Ten years later, she presented her praise dance in church for the first time. It has been applauded everywhere she goes. Her husband, Carl, is now one of her biggest supporters. But the turnaround took ten years.

My husband, Frank, is a tremendous encouragement to me. He supports my speaking and writing. I have become a better person because of being married to him. There are times, however, when I want to do a project and he does not agree. According to God's Word, I yield, and put the idea on the back burner, not knowing if it will ever be done in my lifetime. I have heard women say God called them into ministry against their husband's wishes. That is out of order; God never violates His own rules.

It's important that you understand what you are giving up when you get married. Don't give up your right to make the final decision in your life to just anyone! Take a very serious look at how the man you're interested in makes decisions regarding his own life. If any changes are to be made in his decision-making ability, they should come about *before* you get married.

The wedding vows are unconditional. Nowhere is it said, "I will if you will." Marriage is not a 50/50 proposition; it's 100/100. Your spouse's amount of effort is not contingent upon yours. And there is nothing in the vows to suggest that anyone will ever change. Yet when things go wrong, it's so common to hear, "I knew he had problems when I married him but I thought he would change."

It is wonderful when people change for the better, but no one has the right to "make" another person change. People are what they are. Before you consider marrying someone, you should ask yourself the question, "If this person never changed would I want to spend the rest of my life with him?"

If the answer is, "No!" that should be the end of the relationship.

Divorced?

If you've been through a divorce, you may have felt guilty or ashamed as you reread the wedding vows. Those feelings are understandable, but please remember that "There is now no condemnation for those who are in Christ Jesus" (Romans 8:1).

That Scripture has been very important in my life when I've considered some of my own mistakes.

Although there is no condemation for Christians, there are consequences resulting from every decision we make. Divorced men and women usually suffer from deep grief. They may experience a profound sense of failure. Loneliness and disappointment will probably distress them from time to time. If you find yourself in these circumstances, you can be sure that God will walk through them with you. However, if you have broken the wedding vow and have questions about your future, I suggest that you read the book *Single, Married, Separated— Life After Divorce* (Destiny Image, 1993) by Dr. Myles Munroe. In Dr. Munroe's thoughtfully written pages I hope you'll find answers for the difficulties that are troubling you.

Wedding-Bell Blues

You may have heard about the "wedding-bell blues." That phrase describes the depression that sets in when reality hits newlyweds. Not long after the wedding, a couple discovers that marriage is not a "romantic balcony," it's a "spiritual battlefield." How can a single woman avoid the tremendous disappointments of a "not so perfect wedding," a potentially unfulfilling honeymoon, or the anxiety that sets in once the marriage begins? As the old saying goes, "An ounce of prevention is worth a pound of cure."

Heather was 35 when she married Phil. He was definitely a godly Knight and they had a wonderful courtship. This was a very special time for me because I had known Heather since she was 21. She was determined to remain a virgin until she got married—to wait patiently for the right person. There were late night calls when she would cry and share her frustrations as the years ticked away. Then, at long last, her future husband appeared.

Arriving at the wedding rehearsal, I expected to see Heather floating on clouds. Instead she seemed stressed and irritated. As we were leaving the sanctuary she glanced over her shoulder and groaned, "Look over there! That bow is crooked!"

On the other side of the church, one of the big white bows that lined the pews was tilted slightly to the left. It was then I realized that Heather had imagined her fantasy wedding one too many times. Now that she was experiencing the real thing, even the slightest imperfection was enough to send her to the moon. Because of unrealistic expectations, the joy that should have been hers was replaced by frustration and disappointment.

For a moment, Heather had lost sight of God's purpose for the wedding, which is to state the marriage vows in the presence of friends and witnesses. Marriage is also a physical representation of Christ's love for the church which makes it a glorious celebration. When the event is focused on the people instead of the purpose, disappointment is inevitable. In this imperfect world bridesmaids will sometimes be late, the wrong flowers will be delivered, and the wedding pictures won't always come out just right. However, when the focus is clear, even if the carefully planned details fall apart, there can still be laughter and joy.

Your wedding day should be one of the happiest days of your life, but that will only happen when your purpose is clear. It's fine to design a beautiful wedding, but leave room for mistakes. When the day arrives, savor every moment, enjoy each friend's hug and kiss of congratulations. Let your heart overflow with gratitude toward the Lord for bringing you your Knight, and concentrate on why you're there. The reason for the occasion will be standing at the altar next to the minister, waiting to commit his life to you.

A "Knight" of Discovery

The next thing you know, the wedding is over. All the cake (except the top layer) has been eaten. The guests have gone home. Your special wardrobe has been packed and the hotel reservations have been confirmed. Even more than the wedding, the hours and days that follow are vulnerable to the greatest disappointment simply because the honeymoon is so frequently fantasized. Most couples do not share their fantasies with the other partner—especially not in detail. The problem is that reality can never match fantasy. The smell, the temperature of a room, the weather, even the lighting can all be tremendous distractions.

How can a couple have an incredible honeymoon? The answer is to have no expectations. Well, you can have one—you will be together. But once you arrive at your destination, allow yourself to relax and simply enjoy every moment. Rejoice in the fact that you are away with someone who is committed to you for the rest of your life. Enjoy the simple pleasures of touching, hugging, and walking together. Let each day unfold naturally and savor every moment.

Chapter 5, "In the Heat of the Knight," addressed the subject of sex at length. Many times the sexual union after marriage is viewed as the culmination of everything. However, I prefer to call it the "first night of discovery." You'll be together for the rest of your lives. If you're exhausted when you reach your honeymoon destination, agree that it's all right to fall asleep in each other's arms and enjoy each other sexually when you're rested.

During your first encounter, consider it a great accomplishment to learn just one thing that pleases your spouse sexually, and teach him something that pleases you. If that is your goal each time you have sex, just think how much you'll know by the end of the year! When too much pressure is placed on the honeymoon, many tears can be shed because of unrealistic expectations. If you have it all preplanned, throw the fantasy out the window and allow yourself to be surprised.

The Honeymoon Is Over

The honeymoon should never be over! Since I stated my marriage vows in May 1973, I have become more and more excited about being married to Frank. I've learned the principles of being happily married, I've stopped trying to change him in any way, I've started appreciating every little thing he does for me, and I've learned to savor even the smallest of moments.

Frank and I get up at different times in the morning, but when we finally pass each other in the house we stop and he holds me in his arms. In this unspoken expression of love, I delight in feeling the pressure of his arms around me, smelling his cologne as I rest my head on his chest, and listening to his heartbeat. This embrace probably lasts a minute, but it's as if time stands still. There are many beautiful moments in our relationship and for years they went unnoticed. The honeymoon is not over because we have chosen to keep our romance alive.

Your honeymoon should not be viewed as a brief event but as a lifelong pursuit. Remember when Larry said he didn't start dating Antoinette until they were married? I loved that. Romance should not be the focus for dating; it should be an ongoing commitment to your marriage.

Until Death Do Us Part

The wedding is over, you're back from the honeymoon, and now it's time to settle into a daily routine. If you're not careful, life can become boring because you're doing the same things day in and day out. There's one way I know to keep yourself continually challenged—never stop learning about your husband.

I attend the Frank Wilson University. I am studying for my master's degree in husbandology and child psychology. Two of my main subjects are English and Franklish—of which I am striving to become fluent. English is the language in which I communicate my thoughts and ideas to everyone who speaks the language. Franklish is used in my communication with Frank.

I have learned over the years that it's not only what I say, but it's also how I say it that causes effective communication with my husband. I have purposed to study his needs and desires as intently as I would if I were going for an actual academic degree. I wish I could say I get straight A's, but I have sometimes found myself failing in certain classes and having to start all over again.

What about you and your husband-to-be? Your wedding day will only be the beginning. The vows you say unlock the door to your future. You are entering into new freedom, new adventure, and a new level of relationship—a relationship God has designed to be the most intimate, fulfilling one on earth. Marriage is not the end of a courtship; it is the start of a wonderful, lifelong love affair with your Knight in Shining Armor.

_____ *Things to Think About and Do* _____

1) Meditate on the marriage vow.

2) Since you give your husband the right to make the final decisions in your life, name three things about his character that will be important to you.

   a)

   b)

   c)

Knight
Rider

Imagine a knight approaching on a white stallion. His armor gleams and glistens, reflecting the sunlight. A breathless damsel standing alongside the road watches intently. The knight comes to a halt, beholds the maiden, and extends his hand in an invitation of marriage. She eagerly accepts.

As he pulls her up to the back of the horse to "ride off into the sunset" and "live happily ever after," a bottle of metal cleaner suddenly appears in her hand. She takes one look at the scarred and tarnished armor on the knight's back, and realizes then that he was only able to polish the front! Worse yet, there were gaping holes that would have to be welded. Worst of all (if the knight is not a Christian) there is no back armor and the metal cleaner is bound to burn his bare flesh.

No maiden is perfect. But God created a "helper" for husbands because God knew husbands would need help! Many men have done a good job of polishing up the front of their armor. They make a dazzling first impression. It's only when a woman uses wisdom, patience, and discernment that she gets a good look at the flaws he hides from view.

Bad Reasons, Poor Excuses

Again and again I hear frustrated married women say, "I met him in church and he seemed to love the Lord, so I just figured everything would work itself out!"

Additionally, in innumerable counseling sessions, I've heard the flip side of that statement used to justify divorce: "I thought the Lord had spoken clearly to me about the person I married, but now I see I didn't hear God's voice after all. It's obvious that I let my feelings do the selecting. And since this is not the person God wanted in my life, I've decided to get a divorce. Next time I'll wait for the one God intended for me."

This is one of Satan's greatest tricks. I have watched Christians leave a marriage because they've concluded that they didn't hear God clearly about their chosen spouse. They assure everyone, "The next one will be right." Then, when they are remarried and new challenges arise, they are too ashamed to get help. They find themselves heartsick and confused because they are having so many problems—again. They often suffer silently.

All too often the reason for divorce is not adultery or an unbelieving spouse who chooses to leave. Divorce usually happens because couples are confronted by difficulties they never dreamed would happen between two Christians. Who would have ever thought that people who say they love Christ would experience constant arguments, dissension, rejection, verbal abuse, and deceit?

Unfortunately, the divorce rate among Christians isn't much lower than that of unbelievers. What has caused this hemorrhaging? One of the reasons is that Satan has deceived us with unrealistic expectations for marriage. Lack of preparation in the single life and not asking the right questions during the dating process complicate the problem. Furthermore, our society now offers divorce as an acceptable alternative. Not many years ago, people would join together and try to save marriages. Now they just watch and shake their heads.

Don't Be in a Hurry!

Kathy traveled from Los Angeles to the East coast to visit with her family during the holidays. Her desire to get married was evident in our many conversations. She was beginning to grow weary and disconcerted as she waited for her Knight. Then she ran into her childhood sweetheart and thought she heard the Lord clearly tell her that he was to be her husband. They married that same weekend.

When Kathy called me to report the good news she could tell from my voice that I was deeply concerned. When I asked if he was a Christian her reply was, "No, but I'm going to make sure he starts attending church. There is no doubt in my mind that he is going to give his heart to the Lord. I know God told me he was my husband."

"That could very well be true," I told her. "The question may not be *if* he's your husband; it may be *when* he was supposed to become your husband. Your ability to influence him in a powerful way has been lost, because now you are in submission to a man who is not listening to God. He has the right, according to 1 Peter 3:1, to make the final decisions in your life even though he is unsaved."

"Well," responded Kathy, "I know what God said and I'm going to stand in faith." Six months later the marriage was dissolved. She returned broken and distraught. She learned the hard way.

Reviewing Some Key Issues

As I said in the introduction, you may have read this book in one sitting, but it will take months for you to work out its principles. I hope you've made the commitment to undergo the six-month waiting period. You might find it helpful to have a friend working on "reconstruction" with you—to provide encouragement and moral support. Even if she quits in the process, don't you give up! Push through to the end.

Don't be afraid to seek professional help when you hit the rough spots. As you allow your best friend, the Holy Spirit, to shine a light in the dark places in your life and heart, it may be necessary to join a support group or receive personal counseling. But please make sure you receive godly counsel from a reputable Christian counselor, preferably one who has been referred by your pastor or by a solid, Bible-believing church in your area.

Save some money as you go along so that at the end of six months you and the Lord can go on a honeymoon. (That includes you single parents. Don't feel guilty about spending time away from the children. It will do you both a world of good!) After six intimate months together with the Lord you will have the time of your life. Allow Him to romance you and let you know how much He loves and thinks about you. Relax in the abiding contentment of the Father, Son, and Holy Ghost. Don't forget to send me a postcard: P.O. Box 2601, Pasadena, California 91102.

Once you've celebrated your marriage to your First Love, you'll be ready to meet your Knight. This final chapter is designed to help review what you have learned, and to provide pertinent information you can refer to quickly. Remember the first work begins with you. Make sure you have . . .

- started a six-month journal.
- put a six-month hold on dating.

And that you are . . .

- monitoring your thought-life.
- memorizing Scripture to counteract any negative thinking.

- allowing the Holy Spirit to identify people who have hurt and defiled you.

- taking the steps to forgive, reconcile, and love unconditionally.

- asking the Holy Spirit to reveal the three greatest areas in your life that need to be healed, for example, fear, bitterness, doubt, jealousy, anger, or a low self-image.

- studying your schedule. Have you devoted it to God so you're free to do what He wants?

- listing the ways you would like your Knight in Shining Armor to see you.

- facing up to areas in which you need to grow.

Is He the Man for You?

Now that you are working on yourself, let's take a look at your future Knight. Remember, when speaking to the opposite sex, the goal is not to enter into a romantic relationship, but to uncover the character of someone in whom you might be interested. Within a short time you should know if a man has a personal relationship with Jesus Christ. Encourage him to share his testimony, letting you know how he came to the Lord. Be sure you've heard . . .

- *A clear and definite answer concerning his walk with the Lord.* If he tells you the name of his church it's a good indication he is "churchy," but he may not know Jesus personally.

- *His personal testimony.* Growing up in a Christian household or having parents in the ministry does not make a person a Christian.

- *The name of Jesus.* When a man says he believes in God but does not mention Jesus, he may just be religious. Christianity is not a religion—it is a relationship between God and man through His Son, Christ Jesus.

If a man has not received Christ's pardon for his sins or if he is in a backslidden state, it is not your job to disciple him. It is dangerous to become emotionally involved with a habitual sinner or an immature Christian. If a man appears to have a genuine interest in knowing or growing deeper in Christ, refer him to a godly male or to a men's group in your church to encourage him in his walk. Be up front with him concerning your desire to develop a relationship *only* with a man who doesn't want to break God's heart. His pride and desire to conquer will either draw him to or drive him away from a deeper relationship with Jesus.

Allow the Holy Spirit to do His job without your intervention. If the man begins to show an interest in Christ, allow him at least six months of growth before considering a more serious relationship. If you marry a baby Christian, don't complain when he keeps asking you to bring him formula!

Three Essential Questions

There are three immediate things you want to know about a man when you first meet. All the questions need not be answered in your first conversation, but they should be addressed within a short period of time. Those three questions are:

1. Do you have a personal relationship with Jesus Christ? Please share your testimony.

2. Have you ever been or are you now married? Do you have children?

3. Tell me about your family and your childhood.

We've already addressed the first question. Now let's go to the next one.

The Truth, the Whole Truth . . .

The second question is very important. Be sure you ask, because the man may still be married. If so, hightail it and run! Don't allow yourself to listen to the reasons why he would strike up an in-depth conversation with a single woman. "My wife doesn't understand me" is the oldest line in the book. The second oldest line is "Trust me. I'm not like the other married guys who cheat on their wives."

Donna asked John if he had any children. His answer was no. After they had been dating for three months she discovered he had a son. When she questioned him about not telling the truth he said, "I knew you would be upset and I didn't want to lose you."

Donna was smart. She ended the relationship immediately. John exhibited two tremendous flaws. The first was deceit. If a person lies about one thing, he will lie about another. John felt that if he could get Donna emotionally attached to him then it would not matter whether he had a child. That brings us to flaw number two—manipulation. The truth is, Donna wouldn't have minded if he had been honest.

If a man does have children it is important to know if he is involved in their lives and if he supports them financially. If you marry a man who is not participating in the lives of his children, don't be surprised when he doesn't want to take care of the children you have together.

When I met Frank he had two children. His first wife had died and his daughter was being raised by his mother. She was in private school, and Frank was providing for her care, but she came to live with us once we were married. He was also raising his three-year-old son and simply adored him. Responsibility, dependability, and faithfulness radiated from his character.

If a man has been married, it's important for you to discover why the relationship ended. Remember, there are always two sides to a story. Where does he feel he failed? It's an indication of irresponsibility if he places all the blame on his ex-wife.

Also, what has he done to heal the wounds caused by the divorce? Beware of a man who has unresolved bitterness, anger, and resentment. It will inevitably bleed into the next relationship. If he has not dealt with his feelings concerning the divorce, let him know that you will not consider becoming involved with him until he has received counseling to overcome his bad feelings. I hope this will stimulate him to get help. If not, my suggestion is to move on quickly.

What About His Past?

Pay close attention to your potential Knight when you ask, "Tell me about your childhood." Take caution if he doesn't want to discuss it or is vague. His relationship to his father and mother is vital. If they were not good role models for marriage, you can expect him to duplicate their actions in your relationship. Just because a man has a poor relationship with his mother or father does not mean he should be discounted. However, you would want to encourage him to seek help in resolving any ongoing differences.

In a recent movie, a man went to his sister's psychiatrist to find out why his sister kept trying to commit suicide. He didn't want to go, but because of his love for his sister he allowed himself to be used to get to the bottom of her trouble. While doing so, he was healed of his own painful childhood. Allow the Lord to use you to stimulate a man who is interested in you to seek godly counsel concerning his personal challenges.

Meanwhile, do not get emotionally involved. It is important for you to be able to walk away from any man who is unwilling to yield to godly counseling. Without counsel, it will be nearly impossible for him to break destructive patterns of behavior and to learn God's plan for a successful marriage.

Points to Ponder

While you're dating, in the midst of the laughter and the interesting conversations, there should be one dominant thought: You are there to interview—to gather data—and not to be romanced. That will come later with the right person at the right time. In the meantime, try not to act like an interrogator, but keep the goal in mind. It would be helpful if you had a friend who could assist you in keeping focused and on track—someone who has the right to ask questions concerning the progress of the relationship. If you find yourself not wanting to talk about someone, it is probably an indication that you sense something is wrong.

Satan is a tremendous counterfeiter. He has men available who seem to know how to say all the right things. Have you ever watched an impersonator? There are certain things they can say that sound exactly like someone else. However, they are limited in the length of their presentation. Sooner or later the real person comes through the charade. In the same sense, if you give the Lord time to reveal the heart of a man to you, his intent and character will become evident.

Once you remove the idea of romance and adopt an interviewing spirit, trivial talks will diminish. Your conversations will have substance and not be insignificant chatter. Sometimes women have a tendency to talk a lot with no real goal in mind; they enjoy the pleasure of talking. Unfortunately, those same women do very little listening. After every conversation or time together, take time for a period of reflection. What did you hear, see, or feel? What good qualities about the man's character were uncovered? Did you notice anything that concerned you?

Listen to the Bad News

There was a song in the 50s that had a line that went, "Don't say nothing bad about my baby. He's good, he's good to me, and that's all I care about." A single woman of wisdom should care deeply about how others view her potential Knight. His apparent good character should reach far beyond their relationship. Coworkers, relatives, and friends should be able to attest to his honesty, integrity, faithfulness, loyalty, kindness, godliness, and compassion. Of course, there may be times when people will jealously share something unkind. Don't discard negative information because someone is angry or disconcerted with the man. If you listen carefully and long enough, facts about his true nature will be uncovered.

Look Out for Past Abuse

It is also important to know if he has been physically abusive in past relationships. In many cases, an abuser will not admit to such a dangerous shortcoming. These are the kinds of things you need to listen for when spending time around his friends or relatives.

If you discover there has been past physical abuse and it hasn't been dealt with, refuse to allow the relationship to proceed until he has successfully completed counseling. This aspect is critical because abuse is an emotional illness that must be treated. Ignore his pleas when he claims he has learned his lesson and will never allow himself to become that angry again. If he wants you badly enough, he will seek professional help. Let him know that you will believe him when you hear that he is well from a trained counselor. Hopefully, because you have chosen not to become emotionally involved, you will have no problem walking away from the relationship if he does not seek and *complete* his counseling. If you don't, it could cost you dearly.

What Is His Sexual Attitude?

Don't forget to pay close attention to his conversations or comments regarding sex. You should want a man who is teachable; your body is unlike that of any other woman. Watch out if a man feels he has all the experience needed to satisfy a woman, or if he brags about his conquests. When the subject of sex arises, allow him to share his thoughts freely. Don't make him feel you are judging him. Collect the information and then make a decision.

It's worth repeating: Stay away from anyone who participates in masturbation and pornography. If it's appropriate and safe for you to discuss his sexual behavior with him, share the truth about these two sexual perversions (refer to chapter 5). He may have a change of heart, but even if he claims he's changed, proceed slowly and alertly. This is particularly important if you have children. Listen and look for any signs of perversion. Ask God to show you his heart.

Insist on Accountability

It is vital that the man of your dreams be accountable to other people for his witness and walk with Christ. What is his relationship with his pastor? Are there other Christian brothers who have the right to challenge him if they are concerned about his actions or decisions? Be very careful with someone who says he is private or appears to be a loner. The way we live our lives as believers should be an open book. If a man is accountable in his single life, it will provide you with the security of knowing he will be open to counseling later on, if necessary.

Does he see the value of premarital counseling? A man who humbly receives helpful information concerning a successful marriage is a gem. A warning signal should sound loud and clear if he rejects the idea. If we are trained for a job or profession, why should it be any less important to be educated, rehearsed, and prepared for a lifetime commitment?

Don't Overlook His Finances

Observe his handling of finances. Does he complain of being in debt? Don't be fooled by a man that drives an impressive car and lives in a beautiful home or apartment. That may be an indication of financial success *or* an overextended credit line. What is his attitude toward money? Are his business decisions based on integrity? Does he have a realistic financial plan? How does he arrive at his decisions? Does he go in the direction he feels is right or does he pray and ask the Lord for guidance? Does he ask you to pray for or with him? Prayer is what will hold a relationship and family together. It's important that a man realizes the power of prayer and applies it to every aspect of life—including finances.

Check Out His Suit of Armor!

Don't be concerned about uncovering weaknesses and shortcomings in your Knight's armor. You will enjoy your greatest amount of influence while you are dating, so the time to strengthen and encourage his reconstruction is *before* marriage. Just because a man has some obvious flaws does not mean he is not your Knight in Shining Armor. No one is perfect.

On the other hand, the only time you have a right to make changes is when you are single. When you vow to accept a person "for better or worse, richer or poorer, and in sickness and health," you lose the right to demand a change. You are then under submission to his leadership. Do you see the importance of identifying and addressing areas of growth prior to romance and commitment? Use the influence God has given you to challenge him to be a godly man. If he runs away, thank God that he left before you were married!

Your Personal Data Base

After reading through the past ten chapters, an abundance of information may be overloading your mental computer. The following checklist is to simplify the process of determining the strengths and weakness of your potential Knight. Over a period of time, you should be able to write a response in each section. Detailed answers to the following questions will create your own special data base, providing you with invaluable information about your potential Knight in Shining Armor.

1) Does he know Jesus Christ as his personal Savior? Write in his testimony.

2) Has he ever been married? Is he divorced? For how long? What has he shared about his past marriage(s) and what is his perception of why it ended in divorce? Did he ever physically abuse his wife? Was he verbally abusive? Write down the details.

3) Does he have any children? How many? Who is currently keeping the children? Is he involved in their lives? Does he support them financially?

4) What do you know about his childhood? If he has siblings, what type of relationship does he have with them? How does he feel about his mother and father?

5) What appears to be the general opinion of him from his coworkers, friends, and relatives? Do they think he's honest, trustworthy, and loyal?

6) What thoughts has he expressed concerning sex? Does he brag about past conquests? Has he shared his opinion on pornography and masturbation? Is he trying to make sexual advances toward you?

7) What have you been able to ascertain concerning his financial condition? Is he in debt? Does he have a financial plan?

8) Who is he accountable to? Are there people who can challenge him in his decisions and his walk with the Lord?

9) How does he arrive at his decisions? Does he pray and ask God for guidance?

10) List his good qualities. List his shortcomings.

11) Describe his response to premarital counseling.

I hope all the data you've accumulated and the information in the preceding chapters have provided you with a realistic perspective of meeting, dating, and marrying a good Christian man.

What Is Your Desire?

Is it still your desire to have a husband? Do you still want to be married now that you know, according to God's Word, that your husband has the right to make the final decisions once you're married? Do you still have a desire to be a wife, considering the fact that you will be required to submit, to possess a gentle and quiet spirit, and to serve?

Jesus said that before we make a decision we should count the cost (Luke 14:28). If you still want to be married, you are now equipped to consider marriage possibilities. Remember, it isn't enough for him to just be attractive, have a good job, and attend church. Evaluating potential mates will be the most important interviews you will ever conduct. Take your time.

Listen to people who can attest to his character. Make sure he is teachable and accountable for his actions.

Are you also willing to remove any time limits on meeting the man of your dreams? Leaving the time to God will eliminate long hours of frustration and discouragement. Let God have His perfect way. At the beginning of the book I quoted Psalm 37:4:

> Delight yourself in the LORD and he will give you the desires of your heart.

By the time you've reached the end of your six-month journey, I hope you will have learned to sincerely delight yourself in the Lord.

True desire is when we allow God to put His desires for us into our hearts. That's when we can rest assured that He will keep that particular promise. After these precious months of intimate fellowship with God have passed, will you still desire to be married? If so, God has a husband for you!

Knight
School

For the past ten chapters, you've been in "Knight School" and now you've nearly come to the end of our time of instruction. You know what that means—once the teacher has presented an abundance of information, you are usually required to take a test to see how much you've learned. Of course, in this case, the true test will take place during the next six months as you practice in a real life "laboratory" everything you've learned. But for now, let's analyze some fictitious case studies and see what you think about them.

After reading the following stories, attempt to pinpoint the strengths, concerns, and challenges each woman faces with a new man. Although my observations are located on page 176-179, I don't claim to have all the answers. You will probably see things in these stories that I missed. That's why I think reading them and thinking about them is great practice.

It's vital for you to learn to objectively evaluate each conversation you have with any potential Knight who comes along.

Case Study 1

Helen, a lawyer, drove her car to Joe's Automobile Service, a reputable mechanic's shop, for repairs. When she arrived, a striking man in blue overalls approached her car. After she explained the problem she'd been having, the mechanic spent a considerable amount of time trying to locate the malfunction. Once he found it, he estimated that it would take about an hour to make the necessary repairs.

Unexpectedly, the mechanic asked, "I couldn't help but notice the notebook on your backseat with the name of a church printed on it. Is that the church you attend?"

"Yes," Helen nodded, "I've been going to that church for eight years."

He smiled. "I'm a member of a similar church about five blocks from here. My parents were members and I've been there all my life. Look, it's going to take about an hour for my men to make the repairs. There's a coffee shop across the street. Would you be interested in getting a cup of coffee?"

Helen hesitated and then shrugged, "Okay." She was shocked to hear herself agree. Until recently, she would have never considered an invitation of that nature from a blue collar worker. She couldn't help but wonder what her colleagues would think if they saw her drinking coffee with a mechanic.

As the two slid into a booth with a red-and-white checkered tablecloth, she noticed her companion's relaxed manner.

Helen asked, "So tell me a little about yourself. Let's start with your name."

"My name is Joe," responded the mechanic.

Helen raised her eyebrows. "As in Joe's Automobile Service?"

Joe chuckled, "Yes, that's me."

"So that's why you were able to leave the work to somebody else."

Joe answered, "That's right. My father owned the business for over 40 years. He died five years ago and I took it over."

"So is having your own car repair shop your lifetime dream?" Helen asked.

"Actually it is," said Joe. "It took me two years of college to discover that my first love was repairing cars. My parents wanted all of their children to graduate from college, and my brother and sister have master's degrees. But I want to do what I enjoy. Of course I'm committed to excellence. And I plan to start a franchise next year."

"Do you ever regret not finishing school?"

Joe responded, "Not yet. I believe integrity, not education, makes the man. I don't measure intelligence by an academic degree. I'm an avid reader and keep abreast of world affairs. And, believe it or not, it takes a lot of knowledge to own and operate your own business successfully."

Helen asked, "Do you live near here?"

"About twenty minutes away. I recently purchased a condominium. I was living with my mother up to that time; she had Alzheimer's disease and I didn't want her to be alone. She passed away a few months ago and I bought my own place."

"How have you adjusted to your Mom's death?"

Sadness reflected on Joe's face. "Not well. I just don't understand why God would take such a wonderful woman and allow the drug addicts and prostitutes to live. I haven't been to church since she died."

The hour went by quickly as the pair talked about their lives. When they returned to the shop and Helen got into her newly repaired car, Joe leaned on her window and said, "I would consider it an honor if you would go to dinner with me."

Helen smiled slightly and said, "I have the phone number here. Let me think about it."

Steering her car onto the street she thought, "What an interesting man. I can't believe he's just a mechanic! I'd like to get to know him better but how would I ever introduce him to my friends?" Helen continued to ponder that last question for a few more minutes. Finally she concluded, "Oh, I know! I'll introduce him as a car specialist!"

What are some of the strengths, concerns, and challenges that should be on Helen's mind regarding a possible relationship with Joe? Make a list in each category:

• Strengths

• Concerns

• Challenges

Once you've completed your lists, see how they compare to mine which are on page 176.

Case Study 2

Kim caught Andre's attention at a professional basketball game. Although she was with two other female companions, she stood out from the crowd. He was immediately attracted to her personality. She rooted heartily for her team, laughed with her friends, and appeared self-assured. During halftime Andre saw Kim standing in line for refreshments and decided to approach her.

"Excuse me," he said.

Kim turned around to see a tall, thin man with beautiful eyes. "Yes?"

In a stage whisper, Andre said, "I hate to tell you this but your team is going to lose."

Kim laughed heartily and shook her head. "Mister, I don't know who you are but one thing I do know is you're confused!"

Andre answered, "I'll make you a bet. If your team wins, you'll never see me again. If my team wins I'll meet you and your friends at Manny's Pizza after the game."

Kim sized Andre up. He carried himself in a calm manner and seemed to have a nice disposition. She didn't see any harm in meeting him at a pizza parlor with her two friends along. "Well, I don't bet so why don't we just agree to the pizza," Kim said as she picked up her popcorn and soda.

Andre and Kim had a wonderful time chatting over pizza and her friends thought he was terrific. They talked about everything from politics to food. It seemed as if they laughed all evening. When it was time to go Andre asked, "May I see you again?"

"Let me think about it," answered Kim. "Give me your telephone number and I'll call and let you know."

Kim decided to have a phone conversation with Andre before meeting him for dinner. When she telephoned, a little girl answered the phone.

"Hello. I might have the wrong number. I'm calling for Andre," Kim said.

The little girl answered, "Oh, you mean Daddy. Hold on and I'll go get him."

When Andre came to the phone he said, "Well, I guess you know I have a child."

"Was that a secret?" asked Kim.

Andre responded, "Definitely not. She is one of my greatest joys. It's just not a subject that came up the other night. I have been divorced from my wife for six months and Nickie stays with me on weekends."

"Oh I see." Kim went on to say, "I was calling because I realized when we left the other night that I knew very little about you. I was hoping we could talk a little more by phone."

Andre replied, "You're a wise woman. So what do you want to talk about?"

"Well," Kim said thoughtfully, "why don't you tell me your life story beginning with your childhood."

"There's not much to say," remarked Andre. "I was born in Oklahoma in 1956 and moved to Cleveland after graduating from Ohio State with a degree in engineering. I'm a manager at Payton Engineering Company where I've worked for 18 years. I have been married twice. My first wife and I had two sons and my second wife and I had Nickie. You're the first lady I've asked out since my divorce."

Kim stated, "You didn't say anything about your childhood? Are your parents still alive?"

"No, they're not, but I wasn't raised by them. My mother wasn't married to my father and she had it hard so my aunt took me in and brought me up with her six children."

"That must have been a lot of fun playing with all your cousins," Kim asked.

Andre replied, "Yeah, but it could have been better. My uncle was an alcoholic."

Kim said, "Oh, I'm sorry to hear that," then gently changed the subject. "So how do you normally spend your weekends?"

"Usually Nickie comes on Friday evening. We rent videos and play board games at home. On Saturday I try to take her to some fun places and on Sunday we go to church."

You could hear the relief in Kim's voice as she said, "What church do you attend?"

"I'm not sure of the name," answered Andre. "It's on the corner by my house. I switched churches when my wife and I got a divorce."

Kim inquired, "Would you consider yourself a spiritual person?"

"Oh, I'm not the best man in the world but I'm also not the worst. Now let's talk about you."

When Kim hung up the telephone and reflected on the conversation, what do you think she wrote on her list of strengths, concerns, and challenges regarding Andre? Would you go out with him?

My observations are on page 177.

Case Study 3

After Tiffany sang one of her favorite praise songs along with the congregation, her pastor walked to the podium and instructed everyone to turn around, get in groups of three or four, and pray for each other. She took the hands of her two children, sitting on either side of her. When she turned around, Jason was standing directly behind her. He smiled at her and the children, took their hands and began to pray.

Three years before, and after twelve years of marriage, Tiffany had lost her husband in an automobile accident. Since the tragedy, she had been convinced that she would never remarry: The pain was too great and she was still struggling with a lot of anger. Only recently had she decided to go through the reconstruction process outlined in *Knight in Shining Armor*. At last she was open to meeting someone.

There is something wonderful about this man, his prayer, and his demeanor, Tiffany thought.

After he said, "Amen," she smiled and introduced herself and the children.

"I'm Jason Trent. You have a lovely family," he responded.

Tiffany asked, "Are you visiting here today?"

Jason chuckled and answered, "No, I've been a member here for a little over a year. I sit in this same seat each Sunday."

Tiffany blushed and stammered, "I'm sorry, please forgive me. I'm not very attentive in crowds."

"I must admit you do seem to have a lot on your mind each week," responded Jason.

Tiffany replied, "It was nice to meet you," and took her seat. After that it was difficult for her to concentrate on the sermon. From what he said, this wasn't the first time Jason had noticed her. She could feel her two children staring at her. They knew something was going on.

Steve was ten and Monica was eight. No sooner had they climbed into the car after the service when Monica asked, "Who was that man in church?"

"What do you mean?" asked Tiffany. "He introduced himself. He said his name was Jason Trent."

Steve remarked, "We saw the way you were looking at him. Don't even think about it. No one is ever going to replace our Dad!"

"Steven Matthew Bond, don't you ever speak to me in that tone again!" Tiffany retorted. "He was just a man who attends our church."

Steve responded, "I'm sorry, Mom. I just miss Dad. I can't stand the thought of someone else being our dad. Please promise us you will never marry anyone again. Do you promise?"

For the first time Tiffany realized just how deeply the children were hurting. She answered, "Steve, there is no way I can promise you that."

Monica announced, "Well, if you get married, I'm running away!"

Tiffany was so amazed at the children's responses that she was speechless. A week later she saw her pastor in the church corridor when she was on her way to choir rehearsal.

"Tiffany," said Pastor Jones, "I have a question for you." She knew that she was looking into the face of a very kind man. He had been a tremendous support to her at the time of Alfred's death. "A church member named Jason Trent has asked me about you. He was hoping you would allow me to give him your telephone number." The pastor looked at Tiffany inquisitively.

"Why?"

Pastor Jones smiled and said, "Well, it's clear he's interested in getting to know you better. Unfortunately, I must admit I don't know a lot about him. He comes to church faithfully on Sunday but he is not involved in church activities."

Tiffany hesitated and then answered, "It will be okay if you give him my number."

The next evening Jason telephoned. "Hi, Tiffany. I was very happy you allowed me to call you."

Tiffany said, "Jason, I'm flattered that you were interested. I'm sorry to have to ask you not to call again."

"May I ask why?" questioned Jason.

Tiffany responded, "I lost my husband three years ago and I don't think I can entertain a relationship at this time."

"Three years is a long time, Tiffany. How long do you think it's going to take you to recover?"

"Well, until six months ago I thought I would never consider another relationship. But the Lord has been healing my broken heart. My concern is the children. I'm just discovering that they are hurting deeply and I don't know what to do about it. They became extremely upset last Sunday when they thought I might be interested in a man."

Jason asked, "Should I take that as a compliment?"

Tiffany realized what she had said and began to stumble over her words. Jason chuckled and said, "It's okay, Tiffany. I was attracted to you also. That's why I wanted to call." He went on to say, "Look, what your children probably need now is some counseling and a male friend who will help them in the transition from the loss of their father to understanding that life goes on. Maybe one day there can be something between us but right now, if you don't mind, I'd like to just concentrate on the children. If it's okay with you, I would like to become their friend first and perhaps in the future, I can become yours."

Tiffany responded, "That is one of the kindest things anyone has ever said to me. Let me think about it."

Jason answered, "Sure thing."

"Do you mind if I ask you a question?" Tiffany asked.

Jason replied, "No, not at all."

"Tell me a little about yourself," replied Tiffany.

Jason said, "Okay. Now let's see, where do I start? My parents were missionaries and I grew up in the church. I was always in church; it's kind of like my second home. My parents and two sisters live in Oregon. By profession I am a certified public accountant. My office is on the corner of Arlington and Duncan Street. I've been there eight years. I'm 39, never been married, and I'm looking forward to getting to know you better."

What should Tiffany list as strengths, concerns, and challenges? My thoughts are listed on page 178.

Case Study Evaluations

Case Study 1:

Strengths

- Helen was referred to Joe's shop because of quality work. That means he is trustworthy and has a commitment to excellence.

- Joe is the owner of a successful repair shop which makes him faithful in business, diligent, and a hard worker.

- He is intelligent and an avid reader.

- He is goal-oriented and is striving to start a franchise within a year.

- He worked for his father which indicates that he has learned submission.

- He took care of his mother until her death which highlights his faithfulness, kindness, and compassion.

Concerns

- Joe's bitterness toward God concerning his mother's death could mean that he is hostile toward God. If so, he will not be seeking God's direction for his life. It may also prohibit him from hearing God clearly.

- Since Joe has not been attending church there is a good chance he has also stopped tithing (assuming he had done so prior to his mother's death).

Challenges

- Helen was concerned about what her peers would think if they'd seen her having coffee with a mechanic. Even though Joe was the owner of the shop, he is still considered a blue-collar worker. Helen will have to deal with her feelings and her pride. Hopefully Helen will realize the most important aspect of a person is character, not career.

Should Helen agree to meet Joe at a restaurant for dinner, what single question should she definitely ask? It could go something like this:

> "Joe, you said something the other day that caused me concern. I find you very interesting, however, my desire is to one day develop a relationship with a man who doesn't want to break God's heart. What do you think it would take to end your hostility toward God concerning your mother's death?

In asking the above question, Helen has used her godly influence to challenge Joe in his hostility toward God. Even if a relationship does not develop between Joe and Helen, there is a good chance he will rethink his decision, thus making him a better man for his potential future wife.

Sometime in the future, Helen should ask about his feelings toward tithing. Once again, if he has stopped or never participated, she should share why it is important to her.

How did you do in identifying strengths, concerns, and challenges? I'm sure you probably noted some points I missed.

Case Study 2

Strengths

- Andre shows consistency, dependability, and leadership in the area of his employment.
- He is taking responsibility for his daughter.
- He has a great sense of humor and is a good conversationalist.

Concerns

- Although Kim shouldn't grill him in their first in-depth conversation about his childhood, it is clear that he was deserted by his father and abandoned by his mother. Also, there are usually emotional problems attached to children who grow up in an environment with an alcoholic adult.

- Andre had been married twice, suggesting a pattern of problems in marriage.

- He gives a strong indication that he does not know Jesus Christ as his personal Savior.

Challenges

- Unless Kim has a tremendous amount of time, I would recommend she leave Andre alone. It could be years before he gives his heart to the Lord and overcomes the emotional baggage that has resulted from desertion, being raised by an alcoholic uncle, and two subsequent divorces.

Case Study 3:

Strengths

- Jason and Tiffany attend the same church. There would probably not be a conflict concerning doctrinal teaching.

- He appears genuinely interested in the well-being of her children.

- He also appears to be putting the needs of the children in front of his desire to get to know Tiffany better.

- He is an entrepreneur with a track record of being in business for eight years.

Concerns

- In the near future, Tiffany should try to discover whether Jason has a personal relationship with Jesus or if his faith has been built solely on the missionary work of his parents.

- Is Jason interested in Tiffany or her children? A single parent must proceed with caution even when the male suitor appears to have a genuine concern for her children. Never forget that almost every child molester is a kind person—that is how they win the favor of the children. As emotionally needy as Tiffany's children are, they could be sitting ducks for a man with a perverted mind.

Tiffany will need to know as much about Jason as possible before allowing her children to go anywhere with him. If his desire is to develop a friendship with them apart from Tiffany, she should send along another male (like a brother) to accompany them. The children should never be alone with him until she is able to accumulate several references that can attest to his good character.

- Jason has been faithful in church attendance but not in church activities. What is his vision for his walk in Christ? What does he feel God calling him to do?

Challenges

- For Tiffany and every other single parent, patience will probably be a challenge. It always takes extra time to make wise decisions regarding a relationship when it involves children.

- Now that it's been revealed how deeply they have been impacted by their father's death, Tiffany should consider counseling for the children, and she should participate in it. Both youngsters need to understand that life goes on. Based on how strongly Tiffany felt about never marrying again, there is a good chance that past comments and responses helped shape the children's thoughts. Tiffany will need to help them through their own reconstruction process.

One More Assignment

During your six-month time of preparation for your Knight in Shining Armor, I know you will welcome valuable teaching tools and will want to put strategic information to work in your life. Every relevant book you read will help strengthen your foundation, reprogram your "receiver and transmitter," and ultimately prepare you for your Knight in Shining Armor. I suggest that you read and reflect upon a new book each month, in the following order.

Month One:
Francis Frangipanier, *The Three Battlegrounds* (Advancing Church Publications).

Month Two:
Mahlon L. Hetrick, *The Money Workbook* (Barbour and Co.).

Month Three:
P.B. Wilson, *Betrayal's Baby* (New Dawn Publishers).
Month Four:
Roger Hillerstrom, *Your Family Voyage* (Revell).

Month Five:
Erwin Lutzer, *Living with Your Passions* (Victor Books).

Month Six:
P.B. Wilson, *Liberated Through Submission* (Harvest House Publishers).

Further Reading:

Bell Ritchie, *A Dad Who Loves You* (Questar).

Gary Richmond, *Successful Single Parenting* (Harvest House Publishers).

Myles Munroe, *Single, Married, Separated—Life After Divorce* (Destiny Image Publishers).

C.S. Lovett, *Help Lord—The Devil Wants Me Fat!* (Personal Christianity).

Verle Bell and Lela Gilbert, *True Freedom* (Vine Books).